Beyond Divorce

DRS. LARRY AND CAROL SNAPP

authorHOUSE®

AuthorHouse™
1663 Liberty Drive
Bloomington, IN 47403
www.authorhouse.com
Phone: 833-262-8899

Published by AuthorHouse 01/22/2025

ISBN: 979-8-8230-4165-2 (sc)
ISBN: 979-8-8230-4164-5 (e)

Library of Congress Control Number: 2025900494

Print information available on the last page.

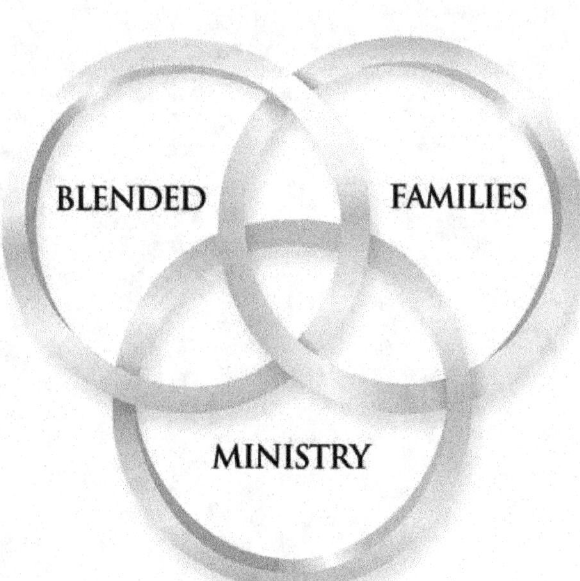
BLENDED
FAMILIES
MINISTRY

Contents

Introduction

The intended audience for this curriculum includes those that have recently had their divorce finalized, those that are trying to deal with having just been served with divorce papers, those that are in the midst of the legal process of getting divorced and those that have not filed, but have been deserted and feel that there is no longer any hope of reconciliation with their spouse.

This curriculum is Biblically based and will use scriptures from the English Standard Version of the Holy Bible to bring the truth of God's word to bear on the ever increasing issue of divorce. Drs. Larry and Carol Snapp have been marriage counselors since 2004 and founded their own Blended Families Ministry in 2009. They created a blended family in December of 1979 and now specialize in ministering to couples and families struggling with "non-first" marriage issues.

The primary purpose of the "Beyond Divorce" curriculum is to help you survive the process of divorce and successfully move on from it. It takes two people to create a marriage, but it only takes one to create a divorce. Sometimes, divorces are mutually agreed to, but more often than not, it is only one spouse that really wants to call it quits and move on.

This curriculum will help you understand the emotional roller coaster ride you are on and is designed to help you take control of your circumstances and reduce the amount of stress you are dealing with.

A few examples of the issues dealt with in this curriculum are:

1. How to deal with becoming an ex-spouse/co-parent
2. How to deal with your co-parent
3. How to deal with the co-parent's new spouse

Eventually, once you get your life back on track and reestablish a good vertical relationship with God, there is a good chance that God will bring someone into your life that He has chosen for you. The Snapps' Blended Families curriculum would be the next step in helping you get your head and your heart right for that special person God brings into your life.

Foreword

We count it an honor to call Drs. Larry and Carol Snapp our friends. We have witnessed before our very eyes the hand of the Lord upon their lives raising them up to minister to the needs of Blended Families. They are true servants with the tender heart of a shepherd.

This book will specifically minister to those suffering the effects of divorce, the pain, the heartache and the misunderstanding. The Snapps desire to bring God's truth and healing. That is their heart in authoring this book. We encourage you to read this book for yourself and share with those you know that are hurting over the pain of divorce. There is healing in His name!

Pastors Arnold & Gwen Tackett
Vessels of Honor

In Memory of Our Friend Gordon West

Larry and Gordon went through a men's discipleship program together starting in 2004 until 2006. For about a year and a half, they met every Tuesday morning for the group meeting. After they were both commissioned to be "Ministers to Men", they decided to continue meeting every week for breakfast, just because of the friendship that had been formed.

After a couple of years, the breakfast club grew and moved from place to place, but always met somewhere. The "club" has been meeting continuously ever since and is still meeting. The Lord called Gordon home about one year ago (2012). He was a true warrior for God. He was always willing to help those in need, offering to fix things. He was a real Mr. Fix-it. You gotta love the true heart he had to serve and be a blessing to others.

Gordon knew the pain of divorce and he would love what this curriculum is going to do. He had struggled with misunderstandings with his family for years caused by the repercussions of divorce. God is faithful and repaired those differences so that the last years of Gordon's life were years of total restoration. He loved getting to do some of the things on his bucket list with his son.

Well done Gordon, my good and faithful servant. We miss you.

A Special "Thank You" To Our Home Church

Dream City Church

We appreciate your confidence in our writing and teaching capabilities. We were honored when you approached us with the opportunity to take on a new ministry that the congregation was asking for. We welcomed the challenge to put together this curriculum in a matter of a few weeks.

"We are the church with the heart", Pastor Tommy Barnett consistently says. We often hear, "Find a need, fill it, and take it to your pastor". This usually means the beginning of a new ministry. Is there any wonder why Dream City Church (DCC) remains the birth place for many new ministries in the community? The Pastors, staff, and leaders listen to the people and search for new ways to render help to its members.

Carol and I are the blessed ones here. This curriculum has opened many new avenues for our already established Blended Families Ministry. We see "Beyond Divorce" as a sort of prequel to the existing ministry. We hope to see a large percentage of folks that go through this curriculum "graduate" into the original Blended Families curriculum.

This curriculum will help you get your life back on track after many trials and tribulations. Once you are whole again, then it will be time to get yourself ready for your new relationship.

We Thank You DCC for allowing us to serve the body of Christ with the gifts God has given us and we pray we can be a blessing to many people that are wounded and hurting from divorce.

This curriculum, we trust, will restore faith, hope and love back into one's life.

CHAPTER 1

The Marriage Covenant and Divorce

One of the very first things we have to deal with when we discuss divorce from a Biblical perspective is acknowledging the fact that God hates divorce. Knowing this, you must be prepared to deal with the consequences of knowingly making the choice to do something God hates. This curriculum will hopefully bring you to a new revelation of who God is, who you are in Christ and going forward, what God thinks of you.

> ***Malachi 2:14-16***
> *[14] But you say, "Why does he not?" Because the LORD was witness between you and the wife of your youth, to whom you have been faithless, though she is your companion and your wife by covenant.*
>
> *[15] Did he not make them one, with a portion of the Spirit in their union? And what was the one God seeking? Godly offspring. So guard yourselves in your spirit, and let none of you be faithless to the wife of your youth.*
>
> *[16] "For the man who does not love his wife but divorces her, says the LORD, the God of Israel, covers his garment with violence, says the LORD of hosts. So guard yourselves in your spirit, and do not be faithless." (ESV)*

Since God's Word tells us that He hates divorce, then why is the divorce rate so high – especially among those who profess to be Christians? Part of the reason is that many who claim to be "Christian" never actually walk it out and are technically still in the world. Therefore, as expected, the percentage is still pretty close to what the non-Christian rate is. It would make sense that "non-believers" would have a much higher divorce rate than "believers". On the brighter side, the divorce rate among "active" Christians is somewhat lower (35-40%). It's still way too high, but shows the application of faith definitely makes a difference.

0First - some things you need to understand about the institution of marriage as established by God:

1. Marriage was intended to be a "till death" covenant between spouses and God – **Genesis 2:24, Matthew 19:6, Malachi 2:14**
2. Marriage is spiritual warfare – trials and tribulations are promised - **John 16:33, Ephesians 6:10-18**
3. God created you with a free will – you can choose to do right or do wrong - **Joshua 24:15**
4. Unbelievers that marry did not enter into a covenant with God - **2 Corinthians 4:4**
5. If God wasn't consulted before getting married, you probably got the wrong one and He has the right one still waiting in the wings - **Romans 13:2**
6. You are not to be unequally yoked with an unbeliever - **2 Corinthians 6:14**
7. If two unbelievers marry and then get born-again later, then God can redeem the marriage for His glory - **Colossians 1:14**
8. If you happen to be married to an unbeliever now that you are born-again, if that person does not want to stay with you, they are free to leave. But if they do want to stay with you, let them stay - **1 Corinthians 7:12-13**.

Selfish things that often lead to divorce:

1. Adultery
2. Abuse of any kind
3. Addictions of any kind
4. Abandonment

Because marriage is spiritual warfare (see #2 above), you need to be aware that you will have to deal with much more spiritual baggage when divorce ultimately allowed to kill a marriage. By choosing to divorce, you are using the law to break something that was only intended to be completed through the death of one spouse.

It should be fairly obvious why God hates divorce, but let's explore some of the reasons. One of the first reasons God hates divorce is that He has personally experienced the pain it causes. Read the words of God, spoken through the Prophet Jeremiah below.

<u>Jeremiah 3:6-9</u>

Faithless Israel Called to Repentance

[6] The LORD said to me in the days of King Josiah: "Have you seen what she did, that faithless one, Israel, how she went up on every high hill and under every green tree, and there played the whore?

[7] And I thought, 'After she has done all this she will return to me,' but she did not return, and her treacherous sister Judah saw it.

8] She saw that for all the adulteries of that faithless one, Israel, I had sent her away with a decree of divorce. Yet her treacherous sister Judah did not fear, but she too went and played the whore.

[9] Because she took her whoredom lightly, she polluted the land, committing adultery with stone and tree. (ESV)

It's important to note that God was always faithful to His bride (Israel) and waited faithfully for her to repent and return to Him. He was always waiting with open arms, grace and forgiveness when she did return to Him. It's also important to understand that Israel would always end up having to deal with the consequences of "her" wicked ways which ultimately led to the repentance and return to God. Being enslaved by Egypt for 400 years is a good example of consequences!

As we saw previously in Malachi 2:16, God sees divorce as dealing treacherously with your spouse. Divorce is one of the most extreme acts of selfishness one can commit (after suicide). In some cases, it is an act of self-defense and would be the appropriate thing to do (see #8 above).

God is a god of generations and He desires godly offspring. When parents do a good job of demonstrating and teaching the Word of God to their children, the blessings continue to flow from one generation to the next. Divorce interferes with the generational blessings God had intended because families are being broken up. Instead of blessings, generational curses begin to be passed on to the third and fourth generations.

Divorce comes from a spirit of unforgiveness. When two people choose to divorce there is some kind of huge offense that seems impossible to forgive. According to Exodus 20:5, we see that this spirit of unforgiveness (iniquity of the fathers) can get passed on for three or four generations to come. After that, the younger generation is much less likely to know about or care about what the problem was that caused Great-Grandpa and Great-Grandma to divorce. Forgiveness is what breaks the generational curse. We will deal with forgiveness in depth in another lesson.

<u>Exodus 20:5</u>

[5] You shall not bow down to them or serve them, for I the LORD your God am a jealous God, visiting the iniquity of the fathers on the children to the third and the fourth generation of those who hate me, (ESV)

The children are the ones that suffer the most from divorce. It often causes them to lose their identity. When there is shared custody, they are always going between Mom's house and Dad's house. After a divorce, they rarely talk about "My" house. The house where a child lives and spends most of their formative years is a big part of their identity. Whatever has ultimately led to a divorce is what has been modeled for the children. This has become their "normal". This is the kind of behavior that they will most likely repeat later in life when things get difficult for them.

In Matthew 19:8 Jesus says that the only reason that Moses allowed divorce was due to the hardness of their hearts, but from the beginning, it was not so. In verse 6, the scripture say not to let man tear apart **what God put together**. An important thing to note here is that you make sure that you know if God put you together with your spouse or did you get married without Him.

<u>Matthew 19:6-8</u>
[6] So they are no longer two but one flesh. What therefore God has joined together, let not man separate."

[7] They said to him, "Why then did Moses command one to give a certificate of divorce and to send her away?"

[8] He said to them, "Because of your hardness of heart Moses allowed you to divorce your wives, but from the beginning it was not so. (ESV)

Marriage is the primary institution God created that gives people an unending supply of opportunities to put His Word to use, proving it is true. When two believers put God's word to the test, the marriage <u>cannot</u> fail. As shown below in 1st Corinthians 13:8 – "Love never fails".

<u>1 Corinthians 13:8</u>
[8] Love never ends. As for prophecies, they will pass away; as for tongues, they will cease; as for knowledge, it will pass away. (ESV)

God's Word never returns void.

<u>Isaiah 55:11</u>
[11] so shall my word be that goes out from my mouth;
it shall not return to me empty,
but it shall accomplish that which I purpose,
and shall succeed in the thing for which I sent it. (ESV)

Marriage was created by God. It should be treated as such.

<u>Hebrews 13:4</u>
[4] Let marriage be held in honor among all, and let the marriage bed be undefiled, for God will judge the sexually immoral and adulterous. (ESV)

Divorce should always be a last resort, but because we live in a fallen world, it has become a fact of life for many. The percentage of remarriages today is accelerating compared to first-time marriages due to the increasing divorce rate over the last several generations.

<u>Romans 12:18</u>
[18] If possible, so far as it depends on you, live peaceably with all. (ESV)

As you go through the lesson, take time to meditate on the various scriptures and use the next couple of pages to journal your thoughts, feelings and emotions as well as the things God is working on with you.

CHAPTER 2

Accepting Your Responsibility

A successful marriage is one where both the husband and the wife are more interested in serving one another than what they are going to get out of the relationship. A successful marriage takes two people giving 100% intentional effort to the relationship. The percentage of intentional effort drops immediately when selfishness is allowed to creep into the relationship by one spouse. One spouse has just crossed over the line from giving into getting. This often leads the other spouse to start looking out for their own self-interests and then the flesh takes over and the two spouses start looking at each other as an enemy. The real enemy is the devil.

> ***John 10:10***
> *[10] The thief comes only to steal and kill and destroy. I came that they may have life and have it abundantly. (ESV)*

This lesson will deal with the following points –

1. Identify the root causes for the demise of the relationship
2. Determine what part you played in those root causes
3. Accept the responsibility for your part
4. Discover what God would have you do now

1. Root Causes

Root causes for the divorce need to be identified so they can be dealt with in truth and love. Anything not dealt with now will be taken into the next relationship and will eventually be certain to start growing again.

To identify the root cause(s) of what ultimately led to the demise of the marriage, there are many things that need to be addressed. Was there adultery, substance abuse, physical or emotional abuse? Was there a problem with finances due to gambling or perhaps the loss of employment? Were there significant health issues involved?

How were you affected by these issues? Whatever the "bad" behavior was in the past has surely created some extremely deep wounds in both spouses by the time couples finally decide to get divorced.

When divorce occurs, it's rarely 100% the fault of one spouse. It's also rare for the split to be an equal 50%-50%. Usually, there Is plenty of blame to go around in whatever percentage it truly is. God wants you to correct the flaws and will continue to give you tests until you pass.

2. What Part Did You Play

It is extremely important that you be honest with yourself and determine what part you played in the failure of the marriage. When you are able to identify the character flaw(s) that you need to improve on, then you will be able to seek God's help in correcting them.

Allowing an exception for abusive situations, there is always something you could have done better that might have made a positive impact on your relationship. Were you setting expectations too high for your spouse to meet? Were you consistently speaking negatively to your spouse? Were you being disrespectful? Were you seen as unloving or uncaring? Did you simply take your spouse for granted? Were you someone that was perceived as always being negative or critical about things?

3. Accept the Responsibility for Your Part

Divorce is the result of one or both spouses failing to fully abide in God's Word and therefore becoming a victim of spiritual warfare. When both spouses are "doers of the Word", they will have a successful marriage – but it does take both being "doers". Confess your sins and God will forgive them.

> ***1 John 1:8-10***
> *[8] If we say we have no sin, we deceive ourselves, and the truth is not in us.*
>
> *[9] If we confess our sins, he is faithful and just to forgive us our sins and to cleanse us from all unrighteousness.*
>
> *[10] If we say we have not sinned, we make him a liar, and his word is not in us. (ESV)*

4. Discover What God Would Have you do Now

You MUST take time to heal from all the wounds caused by the circumstances leading up to the divorce. The last thing God would want of you and for you would be to be caught up in the spirit of vengeance towards your ex-spouse/co-parent. He would also want you to be protected from that same kind of spirit through your ex-spouse/co-parent. Never use your children as a weapon against your ex-spouse/co-parent. It is also important to ask your children for forgiveness for the marriage ending in divorce. It goes a long way to helping them heal as well. They need to know it wasn't their fault and it shows them a good example of God's Grace.

Romans 12:18-20
[18] If possible, so far as it depends on you, live peaceably with all.

[19] Beloved, never avenge yourselves, but leave it to the wrath of God, for it is written, "Vengeance is mine, I will repay, says the Lord." (ESV)

Going forward, you have to get a good understanding of God's original plan for marriage. Know beyond a shadow of a doubt that marriage is spiritual warfare. God's Word provides His children with superior battle gear. If you go into a spiritual battle without the right gear, you are guaranteed to become a casualty of war. Be sure to prepare for battle and put on the full armor of God. With God's armor you know going in that you will be victorious. You do not have to fear defeat. You will never be able to move on in life if you allow yourself to be consumed by how wronged you were by your former spouse.

Ephesians 6:10-20
The Whole Armor of God

[10] Finally, be strong in the Lord and in the strength of his might.

[11] Put on the whole armor of God, that you may be able to stand against the schemes of the devil.

[12] For we do not wrestle against flesh and blood, but against the rulers, against the authorities, against the cosmic powers over this present darkness, against the spiritual forces of evil in the heavenly places.

[13] Therefore take up the whole armor of God, that you may be able to withstand in the evil day, and having done all, to stand firm.

[14] Stand therefore, having fastened on the belt of truth, and having put on the breastplate of righteousness,

[15] and, as shoes for your feet, having put on the readiness given by the gospel of peace.

[16] In all circumstances take up the shield of faith, with which you can extinguish all the flaming darts of the evil one;

[17] and take the helmet of salvation, and the sword of the Spirit, which is the word of God,

[18] praying at all times in the Spirit, with all prayer and supplication. To that end, keep alert with all perseverance, making supplication for all the saints,

[19] and also for me, that words may be given to me in opening my mouth boldly to proclaim the mystery of the gospel,

[20] for which I am an ambassador in chains, that I may declare it boldly, as I ought to speak. (ESV)

As you go through the lesson, take time to meditate on the various scriptures and use the next couple of pages to journal your thoughts, feelings and emotions as well as the things God is working on with you.

CHAPTER 3

Forgiveness

Divorce is not a battle between two fleshes. It's a battle between powers and principalities in the spiritual realm. When two people are at the point where one of them feels there is no hope of reconciliation and divorce is the only option, the enemy of your soul is winning this spiritual battle. You and/or your spouse left your Armor of God in the closet and went out into battle anyway. Without the armor, many things will have been said and done that will leave you both extremely wounded and broken. This creates many opportunities to hold on to grudges and the desire to return evil for evil.

> ***Romans 12:17-19***
> *[17] Repay no one evil for evil, but give thought to do what is honorable in the sight of all.*
>
> *[18] If possible, so far as it depends on you, live peaceably with all.*
>
> *[19] Beloved, never avenge yourselves, but leave it to the wrath of God, for it is written, "Vengeance is mine, I will repay, says the Lord." (ESV)*

In this lesson we dig into forgiveness and then compare the fruits of the Holy Spirit with the works of the flesh. Getting to know yourself from God's viewpoint is a good first step in understanding why we need to be forgiven as well as forgiving. Being able to honestly look into a mirror and see what God sees will enable you to start walking down the path of change. You'll be able to start changing your behavior. You're general outlook on life will improve and the way you interact with others will bless them and you as well. The happiest people are those that have an attitude of gratitude. Through increased knowledge and understanding of what God truly says about you, the healing of wounds can begin. Old and new wounds both need to be laid at the foot of the cross never to be picked up again. Christ died for both the wounds you received as well as the wounds that you caused. There is freedom to be gained by believing God's Word. There is bondage to be suffered by believing the lies of the Devil.

Why Forgive?

When you've committed a sin, it's a sin against God not just another person. You have just put a roadblock in the vertical relationship between you and God. The process of dealing with sin consists of being convicted by the Holy Spirit which produces a Godly sorrow for the sin. Godly sorrow is a deep recognition and understanding that you have done something to offend God. That's different than the superficial sorrow you feel when you get caught doing something wrong. You have to confess the sin to God with a sincere heartfelt attitude of repentance. God will then be faithful to forgive your sins. God forgives and makes a point to erase it from His memory. To Him, it's like it never happened. For man, it's harder to forget, but with true forgiveness, the pain will fade.

> ***Psalms 103:8-12***
> *[8] The LORD is merciful and gracious,*
> *slow to anger and abounding in steadfast love.*
>
> *[9] He will not always chide,*
> *nor will he keep his anger forever.*
>
> *[10] He does not deal with us according to our sins,*
> *nor repay us according to our iniquities.*
>
> *[11] For as high as the heavens are above the earth,*
> *so great is his steadfast love toward those who fear him;*
>
> *[12] as far as the east is from the west,*
> *so far does he remove our transgressions from us. (ESV)*

Most people have an easier time asking God to forgive them when it's just between them and God. It's more difficult for people to let go of things that someone else did to them. Offense is an interesting trap. When you are offended, you want to blame the offending party for "making" you feel angry or hurt. That would be fine if the other party actually had the power to do that. It's your emotion, you either control it, or it will control you. Emotion causes you to <u>react</u> based on how you feel without considering all the facts. When you are the Master of your emotions, you consider the situation fully and then <u>respond</u> based on what you know to be true.

Your normal reaction to an offense is to get even. Scripture clearly tells us that vengeance is only for the Lord to handle. Only in His control can perfect justice be applied to those who offend His children. In our humanness, we are not privy to the ultimate Will of God. That's why we need to take every thought captive, put our "Jesus Glasses" on and respond as Jesus would. The closer someone is to you, the easier it is for them to offend you. It always seems to be the ones you love and care about the most that step on your toes.

Romans 12:19

[19] Beloved, never avenge yourselves, but leave it to the wrath of God, for it is written, "Vengeance is mine, I will repay, says the Lord." (ESV)

When you encounter a situation that creates an opportunity for you to be offended and you pick up the offense, the Enemy now has an open door to inflict more pain and suffering. Every offense against you, when not forgiven, becomes like another brick in your backpack. An offense to you should be seen as an object that's laid at your feet. You have to make a conscious decision to either pick it up and carry it with you or just let it lay there. If you pick it up, it becomes your possession and now you own it. You are responsible for it. If you don't pick it up, you don't have to carry it around with you or make room in your daily life for it to continue to exist.

It's also something you have the option to remove from your backpack at any time to lighten your load. Adding the brick to your backpack is the same as you committing a sin in the earlier paragraph. Before you choose to feel offended, remember what Christ said on the cross in Luke 23:34. Forgiveness removes the brick from the backpack and restores the vertical relationship with God and then He can start the process of healing your wounds.

Luke 23:34

[34] And Jesus said, "Father, forgive them, for they know not what they do." And they cast lots to divide his garments. (ESV)

Forgiveness is something you do for yourself. It's not something you do for the person that committed the offense. Forgiving others is a prerequisite for having your own sins forgiven. As Matthew 6 tells us, we will be forgiven according to the same measure we forgive others and if we do not forgive, we will not be forgiven.

Another good way to help release unforgiveness is to get some helium balloons and write the offense or the name of the offender on the balloon with a marker. Then take the balloons outside and let them go. The rising balloons symbolize giving the offense to God for Him to deal with, relieving you of the necessity to have to carry the offense any longer.

Matthew 6:12

[12] and forgive us our debts,as we also have forgiven our debtors. (ESV)

Matthew 6:14-15

[14] For if you forgive others their trespasses, your heavenly Father will also forgive you,

[15] but if you do not forgive others their trespasses, neither will your Father forgive your trespasses. (ESV)

Later in the book of Matthew, Jesus teaches us that there is no limit to the amount of forgiving that we must do and reinforces the fact that God will not forgive us if we do not forgive.

Matthew 18:21-35

The Parable of the Unforgiving Servant

[21] Then Peter came up and said to him, "Lord, how often will my brother sin against me, and I forgive him? As many as seven times?"

[22] Jesus said to him, "I do not say to you seven times, but seventy-seven times.

[23] "Therefore the kingdom of heaven may be compared to a king who wished to settle accounts with his servants.

[24] When he began to settle, one was brought to him who owed him ten thousand talents.

[25] And since he could not pay, his master ordered him to be sold, with his wife and children and all that he had, and payment to be made.

[26] So the servant fell on his knees, imploring him, 'Have patience with me, and I will pay you everything.'

[27] And out of pity for him, the master of that servant released him and forgave him the debt.

[28] But when that same servant went out, he found one of his fellow servants who owed him a hundred denarii, and seizing him, he began to choke him, saying, 'Pay what you owe.'

[29] So his fellow servant fell down and pleaded with him, 'Have patience with me, and I will pay you.'

[30] He refused and went and put him in prison until he should pay the debt.

[31] When his fellow servants saw what had taken place, they were greatly distressed, and they went and reported to their master all that had taken place.

[32] Then his master summoned him and said to him, 'You wicked servant! I forgave you all that debt because you pleaded with me.

[33] And should not you have had mercy on your fellow servant, as I had mercy on you?'

[34] And in anger his master delivered him to the jailers, until he should pay all his debt.

[35] So also my heavenly Father will do to every one of you, if you do not forgive your brother from your heart." (ESV)

In the era of Grace and Mercy brought to us through Jesus Christ, we have been given freedom from the laws that applied in the Old Testament (see Galatians 5:13-15). Love fulfills the law. However, God's principles still apply. Grace is the gift of salvation. Mercy keeps us from getting stoned (with rocks) every time we do something wrong. In simple terms, Grace is getting what you don't deserve and Mercy is NOT getting what you DO deserve.

<u>Galatians 5:13-15</u>
[13] For you were called to freedom, brothers. Only do not use your freedom as an opportunity for the flesh, but through love serve one another.

[14] For the whole law is fulfilled in one word: "You shall love your neighbor as yourself."

[15] But if you bite and devour one another, watch out that you are not consumed by one another. (ESV)

Do You Act in the Spirit or Flesh?

Men and women have two distinct natures. You are eternal spiritual beings trying to figure out how to live a human existence. Most think the opposite – that you are human beings trying to figure out how to live a spiritual life. You WILL spend eternity somewhere. It's your choice as to where. The default is Hell, so if you don't make a conscious decision to accept Christ as your Lord and Savior, you have basically made your decision to accept the default. As you stroll through Galatians Chapter 5:16-26, you discover two distinct lists that describe each of these two natures. A table following the scriptures makes it easier to see the differences.

<u>Galatians 5:16-26</u>
Keep in Step with the Spirit

[16] But I say, walk by the Spirit, and you will not gratify the desires of the flesh.

[17] For the desires of the flesh are against the Spirit, and the desires of the Spirit are against the flesh, for these are opposed to each other, to keep you from doing the things you want to do.

[18] But if you are led by the Spirit, you are not under the law.

[19] Now the works of the flesh are evident: sexual immorality, impurity, sensuality,

[20] idolatry, sorcery, enmity, strife, jealousy, fits of anger, rivalries, dissensions, divisions,

[21] envy, drunkenness, orgies, and things like these. I warn you, as I warned you before, that those who do such things will not inherit the kingdom of God.

[22] But the fruit of the Spirit is love, joy, peace, patience, kindness, goodness, faithfulness,

[23] gentleness, self-control; against such things there is no law.

[24] And those who belong to Christ Jesus have crucified the flesh with its passions and desires.

[25] If we live by the Spirit, let us also keep in step with the Spirit. [26] Let us not become conceited, provoking one another, envying one another. (ESV)

Works of the Flesh	Fruits of the Spirit
Adultery	Love
Fornication	Joy
Uncleanness	Peace
Lasciviousness (Lewdness)	Long-suffering
Idolatry	Gentleness (Kindness)
Witchcraft (Sorcery)	Goodness
Hatred	Faith
Variance (Contentions or Quarreling)	Meekness
Emulations (Jealousies)	Temperance (Self-Control)
Wrath (anger)	
Strife (Selfish ambitions)	
Seditions (treason or dissentions)	
Heresies	
Envy	
Murder	
Drunkenness	
Revelries	
And the like.	

As you can see, the works of the flesh list is about twice as long as the fruits of the Spirit. You are accountable to God for the choices you make. This list is not a menu from a Chinese restaurant. You should only be picking from Column "B", not "A". It's no wonder that there is a constant battle going on – your flesh against your spirit. Like Paul, you suffer through times when you know right from wrong, but still want to choose the works of the flesh. God is always willing and faithful to forgive these bad choices as long as you are willing and faithful to confess them.

In wrapping up this lesson, consider how valuable self-control is. You can eliminate a lot of grief, stress and heartache from your life if you can become not the Master of the Universe, but merely the Master of your own emotions.

Proverbs 16:32

[32] Whoever is slow to anger is better than the mighty, and he who rules his spirit than he who takes a city. (ESV)

As you go through the lesson, take time to meditate on the various scriptures and use the next couple of pages to journal your thoughts, feelings and emotions as well as the things God is working on with you.

CHAPTER 4

Everyone Needs Time To Heal

This dissolution of a marriage is very similar to the death of a spouse. The difference is that people didn't die, but a relationship did. During the process of ending a marriage, and often even after the divorce is final, there is much carnage and collateral damage that is created by one or both of the former spouses. This all needs to be dealt with and cleaned up.

Healing takes time. Healing occurs in God's timing, not our own. We can help speed up the process by drawing closer to God and submitting to His Will rather than running away from Him. Take a look at the following scripture.

<u>Ecclesiastes 3</u>
A Time for Everything

[1] For everything there is a season, and a time for every matter under heaven:

[2] a time to be born, and a time to die;
a time to plant, and a time to pluck up what is planted;

[3] a time to kill, and a time to heal;
a time to break down, and a time to build up;

[4] a time to weep, and a time to laugh;
a time to mourn, and a time to dance;

[5] a time to cast away stones, and a time to gather stones together;
a time to embrace, and a time to refrain from embracing;

[6] a time to seek, and a time to lose;
a time to keep, and a time to cast away;

[7] a time to tear, and a time to sew;
a time to keep silence, and a time to speak;

[8] a time to love, and a time to hate;
a time for war, and a time for peace. (ESV)

One of the greatest problems with divorce is how the ex-spouses/co-parents treat each other and frequently use their children as pawns to deliberately cause trouble for each other. The children end up being the collateral damage. They are the ones that suffer the consequences. As was mentioned earlier, God hates divorce because it interferes with His plan for the generations.

Take time to let the children process any changes in the living arrangements. Everyone needs to make adjustments. When they are back and forth from one parent to the other, it's hard to remember the different sets of rules. Please remember that even though you may be a single parent, you are still to be a parent.

Don't fall into the trap of feeling guilty about the divorce and try to "make it up" to the children by being their best friend instead. They will need parental guidance now more than ever. It needs to be your house - your rules regardless of what the other co-parent's rules or are or are not. Once divorce is a factor, children often feel they no longer have "my" house. It's either Mom's house or Dad's house. Theirs is gone.

It's important to tell your kids that the divorce wasn't their fault. Let them know they didn't do anything to cause the divorce. It happened because the adults decided they just couldn't live together anymore. The children need to know that you didn't want them to keep hearing the arguing and seeing the many areas of conflict.

Have a meeting with them and confess that you made a mess of things, and ask the children to forgive you. It will help lessen the animosity and make room for them to forgive both parents. Let them know they are loved and never speak badly about the other parent. The children, on their own, will discover soon enough what is true about each parent. Don't make them feel like they have to choose one over the other. They will ultimately resent you for it.

Their lives need to have some sense of "normalcy", which means as little conflict as possible between the adults. Tell the kids that you both love them and want great things for them. If at all possible, maintain as many family-style events as you can, such as movie night, game night, and other fun things together (with you and your children).

Remind yourself that you are a steward of the children and not an owner. Train them the way they should go. Remind them God loves them too. They are truly gifts from God and you only have a little time to teach them. Be as godly as you can, correct them when necessary, but out of love and not anger.

What can you do to mitigate the impact of the generational curses that normally get passed on to the next generation through divorce? The easy answer to that question is that YOU need to take some time to heal from all the wounds that you received and also take some time to get your vertical relationship with God back in order. You will also need to confess all the sins you committed and ask God to forgive you for the part you played in the failure of the marriage that just ended. THEN, you will need to forgive yourself.

Consider this example. Every time you or your former spouse said or did something ugly to each other, it was like pounding a big nail into a wooden fence. If there was never an apology given, then the nail stays in the fence. After a period of time, the nail corrodes and leaves a nasty stain on the wood. If an apology was given, then that is like taking the nail out of the fence. However, once the nail is removed, a hole is left behind.

What has to happen to repair and restore the fence to its original pristine condition? Someone needs to come along, remove the nail if it is still there and then fill in the hole with some putty. It takes some time for the putty to cure and be ready for the finishing process. The finishing process requires some sanding to remove any rough spots before it is ready for painting. It could also take more than one coat of paint to be fully restored.

God is the only one that has the perfect putty and paint for the hole in your fence. The key to healing from the death of an intimate relationship is spending time with your Heavenly Father who is more than willing and more than able to help repair all those holes in your fence.

The following scriptures show us how capable our Lord is to heal our wounds.

Isaiah 53:5
[5] But he was pierced for our transgressions;
he was crushed for our iniquities;
upon him was the chastisement that brought us peace,
and with his wounds we are healed. (ESV)

Psalm 147:3
[3] He heals the brokenhearted
and binds up their wounds. (ESV)

Psalm 6:2
[2] Be gracious to me, O LORD, for I am languishing;
heal me, O LORD, for my bones are troubled. (ESV)

Psalm 30:2
[2] O LORD my God, I cried to you for help,
and you have healed me. (ESV)

Psalm 41:4
[4] As for me, I said, "O LORD, be gracious to me;
heal me, for I have sinned against you!" (ESV)

Jeremiah 17:14
[14] Heal me, O LORD, and I shall be healed;
save me, and I shall be saved, for you are my praise. (ESV)

Jeremiah 30:17
[17] For I will restore health to you,
and your wounds I will heal,
declares the LORD,
because they have called you an outcast:
'It is Zion, for whom no one cares!' (ESV)

Matthew 4:23
Jesus Ministers to Great Crowds

[23] And he went throughout all Galilee, teaching in their synagogues and proclaiming the gospel of the kingdom and healing every disease and every affliction among the people. (ESV)

Matthew 8:7
[7] And he said to him, "I will come and heal him." (ESV)

Luke 9:11
[11] When the crowds learned it, they followed him, and he welcomed them and spoke to them of the kingdom of God and cured those who had need of healing. (ESV)

One of the more challenging scriptures deals with how a Christian should treat an "enemy". More often than not, ex-spouses tend to think of their former spouse as an adversary. In the Old Testament, it was "love your neighbor, but hate your enemy". In the New Testament, Jesus had a different approach.

Matthew 5:43-44
Love Your Enemies

[43] "You have heard that it was said, 'You shall love your neighbor and hate your enemy.'

[44] But I say to you, Love your enemies and pray for those who persecute you,

[45] so that you may be sons of your Father who is in heaven. For he makes his sun rise on the evil and on the good, and sends rain on the just and on the unjust. (ESV)

One of the bigger problems people have when they try to start over with a new relationship is interference from an ex-spouse/co-parent. Particularly one that is non-Christian. It is your responsibility as a Christian to NOT be the vindictive ex-spouse/co-parent that often leads to the failure of yet another marriage. Do not let your flesh be your guide. The Holy Spirit needs to be in charge. You don't want to spend any more time than necessary looking into your rear-view mirror trying to fix your past. Keep looking ahead and stay close to God to find out what sort of abundant life He had in mind for you.

Take as much time as you need to heal from the ugliness of divorce before you attempt to enter into a new relationship. Give your children time to heal. Christian counseling for yourself and your children individually as well as all together would be wise. Asking your children to forgive you for your part in the divorce will go a long way towards freeing them up from a spirit of unforgiveness which could lead to another generation cursed.

When you do feel you are ready to move on to another relationship, be sure to get premarital counseling that deals specifically with blended family issues.

As you go through the lesson, take time to meditate on the various scriptures and use the next couple of pages to journal your thoughts, feelings and emotions as well as the things God is working on with you.

CHAPTER 5

Repairing Your Vertical Relationship

If you've just gone through a divorce or your relationship is headed over the cliff, seemingly with no hope of saving it, you will undoubtedly have created a certain amount of spiritual baggage along the way. You will either have done things you will regret later, or you will have been wounded beyond what you felt you were able to bear during the time prior to the divorce. In other words, there will have been sins committed by you and your now (or soon-to-be) ex-spouse/co-parent that ultimately led up to the situation you find yourself now.

Those sins cause a disruption in your vertical relationship with God. God, in His righteousness, can have no part in your sinfulness. In order for you to reconnect with God, you need to repair your vertical relationship. That requires confession of sin and repentance. Let's look at what King David did in Psalm 51 to rebuild his vertical relationship with God. Feel free to use your favorite version of the Bible.

Psalm 51

Create in Me a Clean Heart, O God

To the choirmaster. A Psalm of David, when Nathan the prophet went to him, after he had gone in to Bathsheba.

[1] Have mercy on me, O God,
according to your steadfast love;
according to your abundant mercy
blot out my transgressions.

[2] Wash me thoroughly from my iniquity,
and cleanse me from my sin!

[3] For I know my transgressions,
and my sin is ever before me.

[4] Against you, you only, have I sinned
and done what is evil in your sight,
so that you may be justified in your words
and blameless in your judgment.

[5] Behold, I was brought forth in iniquity,
and in sin did my mother conceive me.

[6] Behold, you delight in truth in the inward being,
and you teach me wisdom in the secret heart.

[7] Purge me with hyssop, and I shall be clean;
wash me, and I shall be whiter than snow.

[8] Let me hear joy and gladness;
let the bones that you have broken rejoice.

[9] Hide your face from my sins,
and blot out all my iniquities.

[10] Create in me a clean heart, O God,
and renew a right spirit within me.

[11] Cast me not away from your presence,
and take not your Holy Spirit from me.

[12] Restore to me the joy of your salvation,
and uphold me with a willing spirit.

[13] Then I will teach transgressors your ways,
and sinners will return to you.

[14] Deliver me from bloodguiltiness, O God,
O God of my salvation,
and my tongue will sing aloud of your righteousness.

[15] O Lord, open my lips,
and my mouth will declare your praise.

[16] For you will not delight in sacrifice, or I would give it;
you will not be pleased with a burnt offering.

[17] The sacrifices of God are a broken spirit;
a broken and contrite heart, O God, you will not despise.

[18] Do good to Zion in your good pleasure;
build up the walls of Jerusalem;

[19] then will you delight in right sacrifices,
in burnt offerings and whole burnt offerings;
then bulls will be offered on your altar. (ESV)

Reconnecting with God is going to be your only true way to move forward in life. You will not want to go through life being chained to the baggage of your past. Vertical simply means up and down. This represents your personal relationship with your Lord and Savior, Jesus Christ.

Society (the world) has gotten to the point where divorce is no big deal. However, in a lot of churches, anyone that has divorced is looked at with condemnation and judgment. The fact that God hates divorce gives the more legalistic folks something to chew on when they find out you have become a statistic. However, where sin abounds, the Grace of God abounds that much more. Also – when you are "in" Christ – there is no longer any condemnation. You just have to have the faith to believe you are free.

<u>Romans 5:19-21</u>
[19] For as by the one man's disobedience the many were made sinners, so by the one man's obedience the many will be made righteous.

[20] Now the law came in to increase the trespass, but where sin increased, grace abounded all the more,

[21] so that, as sin reigned in death, grace also might reign through righteousness leading to eternal life through Jesus Christ our Lord. (ESV)

<u>Romans 8:1-2</u>
Life in the Spirit

[1] There is therefore now no condemnation for those who are in Christ Jesus.

[2] For the law of the Spirit of life has set you free in Christ Jesus from the law of sin and death. (ESV)

When it comes to divorce, you want to make sure you show any children involved that you are working on your vertical relationship and not focusing on what your ex-spouse is doing. Your responsibility to the children is to be a good example. Show them what grace, mercy and forgiveness look like. Do not speak evil of the ex-spouse especially in front of the children. It is best to allow the children to figure out the good and the bad about their other biological parent for themselves. They will need to be able to forgive them later.

In this lesson, we will concentrate on ways to get better acquainted with all three members of the Holy Trinity - our Heavenly Father, Jesus Christ and the Holy Spirit. Father God is our Provider, Jesus Christ is our Lord and Savior and the Holy Spirit is our teacher and guide.

These relationships are based on faith.

> ***Hebrews 10:37-38***
> *[37] For, "Yet a little while, and the coming one will come and will not delay;*
>
> *[38] but my righteous one shall live by faith, and if he shrinks back, my soul has no pleasure in him." (ESV)*

Faith is believing in things we can't see.

> ***Hebrews 11:1***
> *By Faith*
>
> *[1] Now faith is the assurance of things hoped for, the conviction of things not seen. (ESV)*

> ***Hebrews 11:3 -***
> *[3] By faith we understand that the universe was created by the word of God, so that what is seen was not made out of things that are visible. (ESV)*

We must have faith that Jesus Christ died on the Cross for our sins and rose from the dead in three days. We are saved by Grace alone, through Faith alone, in Christ alone.

> ***John 14:6***
> *[6] Jesus said to him, "I am the way, and the truth, and the life. No one comes to the Father except through me. (ESV)*

> ***John 3:16***
> *For God So Loved the World*
> *[16] "For God so loved the world, that he gave his only Son, that whoever believes in him should not perish but have eternal life. (ESV)*

The only sin that will keep us out of Heaven is the sin of unbelief. God doesn't want any of us to perish, so He sent His Son to pay the price for all of our sins.

> ***John 3:17-21***
> *[17] For God did not send his Son into the world to condemn the world, but in order that the world might be saved through him.*

[18] Whoever believes in him is not condemned, but whoever does not believe is condemned already, because he has not believed in the name of the only Son of God.

[19] And this is the judgment: the light has come into the world, and people loved the darkness rather than the light because their works were evil.

[20] For everyone who does wicked things hates the light and does not come to the light, lest his works should be exposed.

[21] But whoever does what is true comes to the light, so that it may be clearly seen that his works have been carried out in God." (ESV)

The vertical relationship can only be achieved and maintained through faith. We are not saved by our works but rather to do good works. Without good works, we can't prove our faith.

Matthew 5:16
[16] In the same way, let your light shine before others, so that they may see your good works and give glory to your Father who is in heaven. (ESV)

James 2:20
[20] Do you want to be shown, you foolish person, that faith apart from works is useless? (ESV)

James 2:26
[26] For as the body apart from the spirit is dead, so also faith apart from works is dead. (ESV)

Faith is just the beginning of our vertical relationship. Building and strengthening this relationship requires prayer and fasting. Prayer enhances intimacy on three levels. It builds intimacy with the one you pray to (Father God in the name of Jesus), the one you pray with (your spouse and family) and the ones you pray for (family, friends and leaders, etc).

Fasting is a time of abstaining from food, drink, sex or even some sort of technology that we can't seem to live without to be more highly focused during a period of spiritual growth. In other words, we humble ourselves by denying something of the flesh to glorify God, enhance our spirit, and get closer to God in our prayer life. Let's look at what Jesus taught in Matthew Chapter 6 about prayer and fasting.

Jesus' Teaching on Prayer

Matthew 6:5-15
The Lord's Prayer

[5] "And when you pray, you must not be like the hypocrites. For they love to stand and pray in the synagogues and at the street corners, that they may be seen by others. Truly, I say to you, they have received their reward.

[6] But when you pray, go into your room and shut the door and pray to your Father who is in secret. And your Father who sees in secret will reward you.

[7] "And when you pray, do not heap up empty phrases as the Gentiles do, for they think that they will be heard for their many words.

[8] Do not be like them, for your Father knows what you need before you ask him.

[9] Pray then like this:
"Our Father in heaven,
hallowed be your name.

[10] Your kingdom come, your will be done,
on earth as it is in heaven.

[11] Give us this day our daily bread,

[12] and forgive us our debts, as we also have forgiven our debtors.

[13] And lead us not into temptation, but deliver us from evil.

[14] For if you forgive others their trespasses, your heavenly Father will also forgive you,

[15] but if you do not forgive others their trespasses, neither will your Father forgive your trespasses. (ESV)

Jesus' Teaching on Fasting

<u>Matthew 6:16-18</u>
Fasting

[16] "And when you fast, do not look gloomy like the hypocrites, for they disfigure their faces that their fasting may be seen by others. Truly, I say to you, they have received their reward.

[17] But when you fast, anoint your head and wash your face,

[18] that your fasting may not be seen by others but by your Father who is in secret. And your Father who sees in secret will reward you. (ESV)

Once again we should strive to imitate Christ. He often got away by Himself to pray in solitude. He says "when" you pray and fast, so it is assumed that they will both be part of your ongoing relationship with Him. Don't forget to listen for His voice during your prayer time. The vertical relationship goes both ways. You talk to Him, He talks to you. Be sure to have your antenna up and the dial tuned to the right station.

As you go through the lesson, take time to meditate on the various scriptures and use the next couple of pages to journal your thoughts, feelings and emotions as well as the things God is working on with you.

CHAPTER 6

Are You Ready for God's Will in Your Life?

Hopefully, by now, you are getting stronger in your vertical relationship so that you are able to focus on and believe in your heart what the Word of God says about you and His relationship with you. It is time to grab ahold of the reality of spiritual warfare and be prepared for battle every day. God is a very jealous god. He wants ALL of you, not just a little here and there.

Exodus 20:4-6

[4] "You shall not make for yourself a carved image, or any likeness of anything that is in heaven above, or that is in the earth beneath, or that is in the water under the earth.

[5] You shall not bow down to them or serve them, for I the LORD your God am a jealous God, visiting the iniquity of the fathers on the children to the third and the fourth generation of those who hate me,

[6] but showing steadfast love to thousands of those who love me and keep my commandments. (ESV)

God wants His children to grow up and be spiritually mature. You need to be a student of the Word – a doer – not just a hearer. He wants you to be able to really chew on the meat of the Word and not just be bottle-fed milk by someone else all the time. You as a Christian are responsible for getting the Word inside you and have it in your head as well as your heart.

James 1:21-23

[21] Therefore put away all filthiness and rampant wickedness and receive with meekness the implanted word, which is able to save your souls.

[22] But be doers of the word, and not hearers only, deceiving yourselves.

[23] For if anyone is a hearer of the word and not a doer, he is like a man who looks intently at his natural face in a mirror. (ESV)

1 Corinthians 3:2
[2] I fed you with milk, not solid food, for you were not ready for it. And even now you are not yet ready, (ESV)

Hebrews 5:12-14
[12] For though by this time you ought to be teachers, you need someone to teach you again the basic principles of the oracles of God. You need milk, not solid food,

[13] for everyone who lives on milk is unskilled in the word of righteousness, since he is a child.

[14] But solid food is for the mature, for those who have their powers of discernment trained by constant practice to distinguish good from evil. (ESV)

Spiritual warfare is real. You have to have an understanding that there is an enemy out there that wants to kill you. Life as a Christian is a daily battle in and for the Kingdom of God. You, as followers of Christ, have chosen to enlist in His army. Ephesians 6:11-20 was mentioned in an earlier lesson referencing spiritual warfare. If you don't put your armor on, you are guaranteed to become a casualty.

John 10:9-11
[9] I am the door. If anyone enters by me, he will be saved and will go in and out and find pasture.

[10] The thief comes only to steal and kill and destroy. I came that they may have life and have it abundantly.

[11] I am the good shepherd. The good shepherd lays down his life for the sheep. (ESV)

Once you fully grasp the concept of the spiritual battle going on for God's Kingdom and know that you need to prepare for battle, you can move on to the fact that God has a great future in mind for you – but first, you have to be seeking God's Will and how you can serve in the Kingdom. Once you gave your life to Christ, you became a citizen of the Kingdom of God. Now, it is time to start living like a citizen of this new Kingdom.

Jeremiah 29:11
Jeremiah 29:11

[11] For I know the plans I have for you, declares the LORD, plans for welfare and not for evil, to give you a future and a hope. (ESV)

Matthew 6:33

[33] But seek first the kingdom of God and his righteousness, and all these things will be added to you. (ESV)

Having now realigned your vertical relationship with God and knowing that each and every day God gives you is another day to put on your Armor of God and go out to battle for His Kingdom it is now time to work on discovering your purpose for which God created you. God's Grace is sufficient to get you through anything the world throws at you.

You have survived the trials and tribulations that have been allowed in your life. Some were due to satanic attacks and some just because of your own fleshly nature. As a child of God and follower of Christ, you are a guaranteed victor. You no longer need to be a victim tied to the sins of your past. Christ died for those sins. What the Devil had in mind to disqualify you from an abundant life, God will redeem and use that very thing to qualify you to serve Him and help others.

To know God's Will for your life, you have to know God and how God sees you. Since you are a citizen of God's Kingdom, it's important to develop a Kingdom perspective on life and the circumstances that come up on a daily basis.

Take a look at these scriptures:

Philippians 4:12-13

[12] I know how to be brought low, and I know how to abound. In any and every circumstance, I have learned the secret of facing plenty and hunger, abundance and need.

[13] I can do all things through him who strengthens me. (ESV)

Romans 8:28

[28] And we know that for those who love God all things work together for good, for those who are called according to his purpose. (ESV)

2 Corinthians 5:17

[17] Therefore, if anyone is in Christ, he is a new creation. The old has passed away; behold, the new has come. (ESV)

Revelation 21:3-5

[3] And I heard a loud voice from the throne saying, "Behold, the dwelling place of God is with man. He will dwell with them, and they will be his people, and God himself will be with them as their God.

[4] He will wipe away every tear from their eyes, and death shall be no more, neither shall there be mourning, nor crying, nor pain anymore, for the former things have passed away."

[5] And he who was seated on the throne said, "Behold, I am making all things new." Also he said, "Write this down, for these words are trustworthy and true." (ESV)

2 Corinthians 12:8-10

[8] Three times I pleaded with the Lord about this, that it should leave me.

[9] But he said to me, "My grace is sufficient for you, for my power is made perfect in weakness." Therefore I will boast all the more gladly of my weaknesses, so that the power of Christ may rest upon me.

[10] For the sake of Christ, then, I am content with weaknesses, insults, hardships, persecutions, and calamities. For when I am weak, then I am strong. (ESV)

Romans 8:1-2

Life in the Spirit

[1] There is therefore now no condemnation for those who are in Christ Jesus.

[2] For the law of the Spirit of life has set you free in Christ Jesus from the law of sin and death. (ESV)

As you go through the lesson, take time to meditate on the various scriptures and use the next couple of pages to journal your thoughts, feelings and emotions as well as the things God is working on with you.

CHAPTER 7

Grieving the Death of Your Relationship

When a marriage ends in divorce, a death occurs. It's not the death of a spouse as when the "till death do us part" covenant has been fulfilled, but the marriage died. Both spouses (and any children involved) now need to go through the grieving process in order to get healthy vertically. If, when you decide to start over, being whole (healed) will allow you to avoid dragging a bunch of spiritual baggage into your new season.

Therefore, each party involved in the divorce needs to go through the same grieving process steps outlined below. However, the warning here is that many times, people either do not know about this "process" or they refuse to go through it. In some cases, people will start going through it but do not fully complete it. Also, the amount of time it takes to go through the process varies from person to person. There is no particular amount of time required to go through the process. Each individual has to find their own way through the process.

In this lesson, we will go through the 7 stages of grief and the grieving process together. They include shock, denial, anger, bargaining, depression, testing, and acceptance. This process is necessary for people to heal after experiencing loss. Keep in mind, each loss impacts an individual in a very personal way. Also, some losses are very sudden, as from some sort of random accident or unforeseen medical issue. Others are due to long-term illness

1. Shock: This stage generally presents itself as what looks like no response at all. A numbed disbelief such that a person just can't believe the news they've just heard that someone close to them has just died. It may serve as an emotional buffer to prevent someone from feeling overwhelmed at the news. You may begin to grieve as the shock and numbness subside.
2. Denial: Where shock is the initial disbelief that the loss has occurred, Denial is the mental state of refusing to accept the reality of the loss. Once an individual accepts reality, they can start actually moving forward through the healing process. Shock and denial help people manage the immediate aftermath of a loss.
3. Anger: This stage can be the most difficult, not only for the person directly impacted by the loss, but the friends and family that are often the recipient of the angry outbursts. An individual often directs their anger toward the person who died, the doctor(s) that treated the deceased, and the hospital where the deceased died, family members, or even

God for not healing the deceased. This emotional state replaces the numbness of shock and denial. It is vital to address the anger. Otherwise, even more damage can occur to the individual or others.

4. Bargaining: Bargaining is the stage where the person that suffered the loss starts trying to make deals with God. These deals often include prayers asking God to remove the hurt and then I'll… In most cases, the deal being offered to God is that "when" He fixes their problem they will make a big change in their behavior, involves thoughts such as "I will do anything if you take away the pain." This stage may come at any point within the grieving process. Guilt frequently accompanies it.
5. Depression: Depression is the stage where it often feels like the weight of the world is on your shoulders. The pain of the loss can be so severe, that just living has become difficult. Normal daily activities have become difficult. There is practically zero motivation to do anything. At this stage, people may experience feelings of emptiness and intense sadness. While this stage is very difficult, it is a step that everyone must take toward their healing.
6. Testing: Testing, as the name implies, is the phase when the person that experienced the loss starts experimenting with a variety of ways to deal with their pain from the loss. It is likely that this person will drift in and out of some of the other phases during this process. It is very important to remember that everyone's journey through this grieving process is unique to them.
7. Acceptance: Acceptance is the final stage of the grieving process. It doesn't mean you are completely healed. It just means that you have come to a place where your new reality no longer has your loved one in it. No one is going to all of a sudden be happy about the situation just because they've finally reached this phase in the process. At this point, you should understand that life will go on, even though it will be very different going forward. Depending on the person, this could be a time of redefining certain roles and responsibilities in this new season of life. New relationships could be formed. A new marriage could happen. Now that we have looked at the individual phases of the grieving process, Let's look at some scriptures that give us a good idea of how God is always there for us in our greatest time of need. We will look at how God can take us through the worst of times and get us to a place where the blessings are abundant.

It's OK to grieve

<u>Isaiah 53:4-6</u>

[4] Surely he has borne our griefs and carried our sorrows; yet we esteemed him stricken, smitten by God, and afflicted.

[5] But he was pierced for our transgressions; he was crushed for our iniquities; upon him was the chastisement that brought us peace, and with his wounds we are healed.

[6] All we like sheep have gone astray; we have turned—every one—to his own way; and the LORD has laid on him the iniquity of us all. (ESV)"

<u>Psalm 31:9</u>

"Be gracious to me, O Lord, for I am in distress; my eye is wasted from grief; my soul and my body also." (ESV)

<u>Matthew 5:1-4</u>

"Seeing the crowds, he went up on the mountain, and when he sat down, his disciples came to him. And he opened his mouth and taught them, saying: "Blessed are the poor in spirit, for theirs is the kingdom of heaven. "Blessed are those who mourn, for they shall be comforted." (ESV)

<u>John 16:20</u>

"Truly, truly, I say to you, you will weep and lament, but the world will rejoice. You will be sorrowful, but your sorrow will turn into joy." (ESV)

<u>Lamentations 3:31-32</u>

"For the Lord will not cast off forever, but, though he cause grief, he will have compassion according to the abundance of his steadfast love;" (ESV)

<u>Isaiah 53:4</u>

Surely he has borne our griefs and carried our sorrows; yet we esteemed him stricken, smitten by God, and afflicted." (ESV)

God is with You

<u>Psalm 31:9-10</u>

[9] Be gracious to me, O LORD, for I am in distress; my eye is wasted from grief; my soul and my body also.

[10] For my life is spent with sorrow, and my years with sighing; my strength fails because of my iniquity,and my bones waste away. (ESV)

<u>Psalm 23:1-6</u>

"A Psalm of David. The Lord is my shepherd; I shall not want. He makes me lie down in green pastures. He leads me beside still waters. He restores my soul. He leads me in paths of righteousness for his name's sake. Even though I walk through the valley of the shadow of death, I will fear no evil, for you are with me; your rod and your

Psalm 55:22
[22] "Cast your burden on the Lord, and he will sustain you; he will never permit the righteous to be moved." (ESV)

Psalm 46:1
[1] "To the choirmaster. Of the Sons of Korah. According to Alamoth. A Song. God is our refuge and strength, a very present help in trouble." (ESV)

Psalm 46:10
[10] "Be still, and know that I am God. I will be exalted among the nations, I will be exalted in the earth!" (ESV)

Psalm 9:9
[9]"The Lord is a stronghold for the oppressed, a stronghold in times of trouble." (ESV)

God is Your Comforter

Revelation 21:4
[4] "He will wipe away every tear from their eyes, and death shall be no more, neither shall there be mourning, nor crying, nor pain anymore, for the former things have passed away." (ESV)

Psalm 34:18
[18] "The Lord is near to the brokenhearted and saves the crushed in spirit." (ESV)

Philippians 4:6-8
[6] do not be anxious about anything, but in everything by prayer and supplication with thanksgiving let your requests be made known to God.

[7] And the peace of God, which surpasses all understanding, will guard your hearts and your minds in Christ Jesus.

[8] Finally, brothers, whatever is true, whatever is honorable, whatever is just, whatever is pure, whatever is lovely, whatever is commendable, if there is any excellence, if there is anything worthy of praise, think about these things.

[9] What you have learned and received and heard and seen in me—practice these things, and the God of peace will be with you. (ESV)

1 Peter 5:7
[7] casting all your anxieties on him, because he cares for you. (ESV)

Psalm 56:8

[8]"You have kept count of my tossings; put my tears in your bottle. Are they not in your book?" (ESV)

John 16:33

[33] "I have said these things to you, that in me you may have peace. In the world you will have tribulation. But take heart; I have overcome the world." (ESV)

2 Corinthians 1:3-4

[3]"Blessed be the God and Father of our Lord Jesus Christ, the Father of mercies and

[4]God of all comfort, who comforts us in all our affliction, so that we may be able to comfort those who are in any affliction, with the comfort with which we ourselves are comforted by God." (ESV)

John 14:1

[1]"Let not your hearts be troubled. Believe in God; believe also in me." (ESV)

Romans 8:28

[28]"And we know that for those who love God all things work together for good, for those who are called according to his purpose." (ESV)

Psalm 30:5

[5] "For his anger is but for a moment, and his favor is for a lifetime. Weeping may tarry for the night, but joy comes with the morning." (ESV)

2 Corinthians 1:3–7

God of All Comfort

[3] Blessed be the God and Father of our Lord Jesus Christ, the Father of mercies and God of all comfort,

[4] who comforts us in all our affliction, so that we may be able to comfort those who are in any affliction, with the comfort with which we ourselves are comforted by God.

[5] For as we share abundantly in Christ's sufferings, so through Christ we share abundantly in comfort too.

[6] If we are afflicted, it is for your comfort and salvation; and if we are comforted, it is for your comfort, which you experience when you patiently endure the same sufferings that we suffer.

[7] Our hope for you is unshaken, for we know that as you share in our sufferings, you will also share in our comfort. (ESV)

Psalm 22:1–5
Why Have You Forsaken Me?

To the choirmaster: according to The Doe of the Dawn. A Psalm of David.

[1] My God, my God, why have you forsaken me? Why are you so far from saving me, from the words of my groaning?

[2] O my God, I cry by day, but you do not answer, and by night, but I find no rest.

[3] Yet you are holy, enthroned on the praises of Israel.

[4] In you our fathers trusted; they trusted, and you delivered them.

[5] To you they cried and were rescued; in you they trusted and were not put to shame. (ESV)

Romans 15:13
[13] "May the God of hope fill you with all joy and peace in believing, so that by the power of the Holy Spirit you may abound in hope." (ESV)

Psalm 18:2

[2] "The LORD is my rock and my fortress and my deliverer, my God, my rock, in whom I take refuge, my shield, and the horn of my salvation, my stronghold." (ESV)

Nehemiah 8:10
[10] "Then he said to them, "Go your way. Eat the fat and drink sweet wine and send portions to anyone who has nothing ready, for this day is holy to our Lord. And do not be grieved, for the joy of the LORD is your strength."" (ESV)

God is the healer

Psalm 147:3
[3] "He heals the brokenhearted and binds up their wounds." (ESV)

Ecclesiastes 3:1–8
A Time for Everything

[1] For everything there is a season, and a time for every matter under heaven:

[2] a time to be born, and a time to die; a time to plant, and a time to pluck up what is planted;

[3] a time to kill, and a time to heal; a time to break down, and a time to build up;

[4] a time to weep, and a time to laugh; a time to mourn, and a time to dance;

[5] a time to cast away stones, and a time to gather stones together; a time to embrace, and a time to refrain from embracing;

[6] a time to seek, and a time to lose a time to keep, and a time to cast away;

[7] a time to tear, and a time to sew; a time to keep silence, and a time to speak;

[8] a time to love, and a time to hate; a time for war, and a time for peace. (ESV)

Romans 12:2
[2] "Do not be conformed to this world, but be transformed by the renewal of your mind, that by testing you may discern what is the will of God, what is good and acceptable and perfect." (ESV)

Promise of Eternal Life

John 16:22
[22] "So also you have sorrow now, but I will see you again, and your hearts will rejoice, and no one will take your joy from you." (ESV)

Romans 8:18
[18]"For I consider that the sufferings of this present time are not worth comparing with the glory that is to be revealed to us." (ESV)

John 11:25-26
[25]"Jesus said to her, "I am the resurrection and the life. Whoever believes in me, though he die, yet shall he live,

[26]and everyone who lives and believes in me shall never die. Do you believe this?" (ESV)

Isaiah 25:8
[8] "He will swallow up death forever; and the Lord God will wipe away tears from all faces, and the reproach of his people he will take away from all the earth, for the Lord has spoken." (ESV)

1 Thessalonians 4:13-14
The Coming of the Lord

[13] But we do not want you to be uninformed, brothers, about those who are asleep, that you may not grieve as others do who have no hope.

[14] For since we believe that Jesus died and rose again, even so, through Jesus, God will bring with him those who have fallen asleep. (ESV)

2 Corinthians 5:8
[8] "Yes, we are of good courage, and we would rather be away from the body and at home with the Lord." (ESV)

Romans 8:38-39
[38] For I am sure that neither death nor life, nor angels nor rulers, nor things present nor things to come, nor powers,

[39] nor height nor depth, nor anything else in all creation, will be able to separate us from the love of God in Christ Jesus our Lord. (ESV)."

As you go through the lesson, take time to meditate on the various scriptures and use the next couple of pages to journal your thoughts, feelings and emotions as well as the things God is working on with you.

CHAPTER 8

Communication Skills

Communication is the number one issue in marriage counseling sessions. There are many ways to communicate - verbally and non-verbally, body language, hand signals, ASL (American Sign Language) to name a few.

In the context of a Godly marriage, we always have to keep in mind that marriage is spiritual warfare and your spouse is not your enemy. Satan is always trying to cause confusion which then leads to misunderstandings and disagreements and all sorts of fleshly behavior if we let him. So, the best place to start is a brief look at spiritual warfare once again. Anything God created, Satan wants to destroy.

The Whole Armor of God

Ephesians 6:10–12
The Whole Armor of God

[10] Finally, be strong in the Lord and in the strength of his might.

[11] Put on the whole armor of God, that you may be able to stand against the schemes of the devil.

[12] For we do not wrestle against flesh and blood, but against the rulers, against the authorities, against the cosmic powers over this present darkness, against the spiritual forces of evil in the heavenly places. (ESV)

Ephesians 2:1–2
By Grace Through Faith

[1] And you were dead in the trespasses and sins

[2] in which you once walked, following the course of this world, following the prince of the power of the air, the spirit that is now at work in the sons of disobedience— (ESV)

Battling Spiritual Warfare

Recognize the enemy

In any kind of warfare, the most important thing is to know your "real" enemy and how they operate. Satan is the real enemy, "The Father of Lies". In marriage specifically, Satan loves to use each spouse as a tool to get the other one off balance and triggered into a bad behavior. At that point, each spouse starts seeing their better half as the enemy and they forget who the real enemy is. So Satan has just won that battle. Who better to use as a tool (battering ram) than the one person that you love the most and that loves you? This approach is very effective because most of the time, the spouses are not prepared for the attack. They have left their gates open and the enemy snuck in.

Use God's Word

In order to recognize a lie, you have to know what the truth is. Satan knows the Word of God better than anyone. His weapon of choice is using God's Word with just a small twist in it to make it sound right and true to most people. But if you haven't been spending much time in the Word, you WILL fall victim to the lies. It's important to recognize that when you and/or your spouse gets triggered, that one of you calls a time out so that you can come together in prayer and do battle in the Spirit and tell the real enemy to "get lost". Get re-focused, come together, pray, resist the devil and he shall flee.

Put on the armor of God

> ***Ephesians 6:13–20***
> *[13] Therefore take up the whole armor of God, that you may be able to withstand in the evil day, and having done all, to stand firm.*
>
> *[14] Stand therefore, having fastened on the belt of truth, and having put on the breastplate of righteousness, [15] and, as shoes for your feet, having put on the readiness given by the gospel of peace.*
>
> *[16] In all circumstances take up the shield of faith, with which you can extinguish all the flaming darts of the evil one;*
>
> *[17] and take the helmet of salvation, and the sword of the Spirit, which is the word of God,*
>
> *[18] praying at all times in the Spirit, with all prayer and supplication. To that end, keep alert with all perseverance, making supplication for all the saints,*

[19] and also for me, that words may be given to me in opening my mouth boldly to proclaim the mystery of the gospel,

[20] for which I am an ambassador in chains, that I may declare it boldly, as I ought to speak. (ESV)

Pray

Since the battles that you have to fight are spiritual in nature, the most powerful offensive weapon you can use is prayer. See Ephesians 6:18 above. Along with the sword of the spirit (verse 17), God has given you everything you need to win the spiritual battles that you WILL face. When you and your spouse come together in prayer and agreement, it gives you a tenfold power to do battle in the Spirit realm.

Deuteronomy 32:30
[30] How could one have chased a thousand,
and two have put ten thousand to flight,
unless their Rock had sold them,
and the LORD had given them up? (ESV)

Another scripture that shows the power of agreement and prayer is

Matthew 18:20
[20] For where two or three are gathered in my name, there am I among them." (ESV)

Clarification - Here's what I think I heard.... Is that what you meant?

We hear words, but we understand based on our belief system or our "normal". Our "normal" is basically the sum total of our life experiences: the good, the bad and the ugly. Some of the past experiences create triggers that we don't always know exist. Often, when the enemy gets in, he will cause one spouse to say or do something that activates a trigger in the other spouse. This is why striving for clarity in communication is so important. Once a trigger is set off, the warfare has begun. It is critical to come to agreement on the understanding of the content AND the context surrounding the idea that is intended to be communicated.

To be a good communicator, it is important to seek clarification of what is being spoken. A common problem in communicating is that we assume too much. Are you assuming positive intent? Or are you allowing yourself to be triggered by something based on an assumption of negative intent?

A very good process for getting clarification on what is being discussed is repetition. As the hearer, repeat your understanding of what you heard the speaker say. This gives the speaker the opportunity to confirm your understanding or rephrase the comment. Giving the speaker a chance to rephrase, allows them to "save face" and avoid the possibility of a misunderstanding. It also helps keep each party focused on the details of the subject matter being communicated.

Scripture References

While there are many scriptures, the most famous Bible verse about communication is

<u>Ephesians 4:29</u>
[29] Let no corrupting talk come out of your mouths, but only such as is good for building up, as fits the occasion, that it may give grace to those who hear. (ESV)

Additional Scriptures Related to Communication (ESV)

<u>Proverbs 15:1</u>
[1]"A soft answer turns away wrath, but a harsh word stirs up anger." (ESV)

<u>Colossians 4:6</u>
[6] "Let your speech always be gracious, seasoned with salt, so that you may know how you ought to answer each person." (ESV)

<u>Psalm 141:3</u>
[3] "Set a guard, O Lord, over my mouth; keep watch over the door of my lips!" (ESV)

<u>Proverbs 12:18</u>
[18] "There is one whose rash words are like sword thrusts, but the tongue of the wise brings healing." (ESV)

<u>Proverbs 18:2</u>
[18] "A fool takes no pleasure in understanding, but only in expressing his opinion." (ESV)

<u>Proverbs 15:2</u>
[2] "The tongue of the wise commends knowledge, but the mouths of fools pour out (ESV)

<u>Psalm 19:14</u>
[14] "Let the words of my mouth and the meditation of my heart be acceptable in your sight, O Lord, my rock and my redeemer." (ESV)

<u>Proverbs 18:13</u>
[13] "If one gives an answer before he hears, it is his folly and shame." (ESV)

<u>1 Peter 3:7</u>
[7] "Husbands, in the same way be considerate as you live with your wives, and treat them with respect as the weaker partner and as heirs with you of the gracious gift of life, so that nothing will hinder your prayers." (ESV)

Proverbs 10:19

[19] "Sin is not ended by multiplying words, but the prudent hold their tongues." (ESV)

Colossians 3:8

[8] "But now you must also rid yourselves of all such things as these: anger, rage, malice, slander, and filthy language fro your lips." (ESV)

Proverbs 18:20-21

[20] "From the fruit of a man's mouth his stomach is satisfied; he i satisfied by the yield of his lips.

[21]Death and life are in th power of the tongue, and those who love it will eat its fruits." (ESV)

Proverbs 25:11

[11] "Like apples of gold in settings of silver is a ruling rightly given." (ESV)

Ephesians 4:15

[15] "Instead, speaking the truth in love, we will grow to become in every respect the mature body of him who is the head, that is, Christ." (ESV)

Proverbs 15:28

[28] "The heart of the righteous weighs its answers, but the mouth of the wicked gushes evil." (ESV)

Matthew 28:19-20

[19] "Therefore go and make disciples of all nations, baptizing them in the name of the Father and of the Son and of the Holy Spirit, and

[20] teaching them to obey everything I have commanded you. And surely I am with you always, to the very end of the age." (ESV)

Proverbs 12:25

[25] "Anxiety weighs down the heart, but a kind word cheers it up." (ESV)

Proverbs 16:23

[23] "The hearts of the wise make their mouths prudent, and their lips promote instruction." (ESV)

James 1:26

[26] "Those who consider themselves religious and yet do not keep a tight rein on their tongues deceive themselves, and their religion is worthless." (ESV)

Galatians 6:1

[1] "Brothers and sisters, if someone is caught in a sin, you who live by the Spirit should restore that person gently. But watch yourselves, or you also may be tempted." (ESV)

Romans 14:9

[9] "Let us therefore make every effort to do what leads to peace and to mutual edification (ESV)

2 Timothy 2:16

[16] "But avoid irreverent babble, for it will lead people into more and more ungodliness." (ESV)

Hebrews 4:12

[12] "For the word of God is living and active, sharper than any two-edged sword, piercing to the division of soul and of spirit, of joints and of marrow, and discerning the thoughts and intentions of the heart." (ESV)

Luke 6:45

[45] "The good person out of the good treasure of his heart produces good, and the evil person out of his evil treasure produces evil, for out of the abundance of the heart his mouth speaks." (ESV)

James 1:19

[19] "Everyone should be quick to listen, slow to speak and slow to become angry". (ESV)

Titus 3:2

[2] *"...to slander no one, to be peaceable and considerate, and always to be gentle toward everyone".*(ESV)

Communication with God

When God created Man, He created man to have a relationship with Himself. God wants to communicate with His people and that His people should communicate with Him as well. The Old Testament records God speaking through a burning bush, a thick cloud, and in a whisper in an audible voice. God wants people to pour out their hearts and share themselves with Him.

As you go through the lesson, take time to meditate on the various scriptures and use the next couple of pages to journal your thoughts, feelings and emotions as well as the things God is working on with you.

CHAPTER 9

Avoiding Post Divorce Landmines

The main objective of this lesson is to let you know that when you more closely follow the word of God, His blessings will become clear. Life won't be perfect, but it will go smoother than it would without God's blessings. An attitude of gratitude will go a long way toward helping you avoid the many landmines that have been planted in your path. Think of it like your real enemy, Satan, is going around planting these landmines where he thinks you might step. One big problem with landmines is that they can lay dormant for years and when you least expect it – BOOM! Something in your life just gets blown up.

The thing about divorce is that two parties have chosen to use the law, to break what was intended to be a "till death do us part" covenant. Therefore, you have now, to some extent, taken yourselves out from under God's Grace, and have put yourselves back under the law. The courts now have a great deal of authority over how you live your life going forward, sometimes for many years.

> **Romans 6:14**
> *14 "Sin is no longer your master, for you no longer live under the requirements of the law. Instead, you live under the freedom of God's grace."* (ESV)

> **Galatians 5:18**
> *"But if you are led by the Spirit, you are not under the law."* (ESV)

When it comes to issues that would require returning to the courts to settle a new dispute, consider the following.

> **Proverbs 25:8**
> *"Do not hastily bring into court, for what will you do in the end, when your neighbor puts you to shame?"* (ESV)

Matthew 5:25

"Come to terms quickly with your accuser while you are going with him to court, lest your accuser hand you over to the judge, and the judge to the guard, and you be put in prison". (ESV)

1 Corinthians 6:7

"To have lawsuits at all with one another is already a defeat for you. Why not rather suffer wrong? Why not rather be defrauded?" (ESV)

Because a divorce is the "legal" transaction that terminates a marriage, the "law" determines how things go for each party. Every state in the US has its own laws to determine how various property is divided up, how custody of children is to take place and any alimony payments that end up as part of the legal agreement. So if you are post-divorce, it is vital that you get proper representation for the state you live in if/when you need to revisit your original divorce documents.

As was mentioned in the first lesson, divorce creates a lot of spiritual baggage that will have to be dealt with eventually. This lesson will help you deal with some of the landmines that become exposed when the divorce paperwork doesn't specifically address them. So the focus in this lesson will be on bringing scripture to bear on some of the bigger issues that often come up after a divorce becomes finalized.

One of the biggest issues faced by both parties in a divorce is the major impact it has on the financial situation of each party. Where two people were living as one household, now, there will have to be two separate households living on that same income. Generally speaking, in most cases, an ex-wife will get possession of the original house and the ex-husband will have to find a new place to live. This often leaves the ex-wife with a house she can't afford and the ex-husband with lots of start-up expenses required to get into a new place. Often it requires the sale of the house to split up the assets. In many cases, the house ends up being sold for much less than it could be under normal circumstances. The divorce decree doesn't always allow for easy adjustments to the official divorce decree. It usually requires spending more money for legal representation to make sure everything is done correctly.

The spiritual baggage is often the most visible in the area of finances. One of the biggest negative impacts is on the ability to pass on generational wealth.

Proverbs 13:22

[22] A good man leaves an inheritance to his children's children, but the sinner's wealth is laid up for the righteous. (ESV)

Another situation where the spiritual baggage is very prevalent is in the shared custody of children. The divorce decree basically just sets the boundaries for shared custody and visitation dates and times. It does not address HOW the two parties are to behave towards one another.

In an intact household, the children generally refer to the home as "MY" home. When they have to go between houses to spend time with the other parent, the houses end up being referred to as "Mom's House" or Dad's House". The children have lost a big part of their Identity. They no longer have "MY" house.

Matthew 5:43-48 tells us to not only to love our neighbors as ourselves but to love our enemies also.

Matthew 5:43–48
Love Your Enemies

[43] "You have heard that it was said, 'You shall love your neighbor and hate your enemy.'

[44] But I say to you, Love your enemies and pray for those who persecute you,

[45] so that you may be sons of your Father who is in heaven. For he makes his sun rise on the evil and on the good, and sends rain on the just and on the unjust.

[46] For if you love those who love you, what reward do you have? Do not even the tax collectors do the same?

[47] And if you greet only your brothers, what more are you doing than others? Do not even the Gentiles do the same?

[48] You therefore must be perfect, as your heavenly Father is perfect. (ESV)

If the ex-spouses have not followed the above scripture (which is very likely) the fallout will often cause one or both of the parents to use the children as a weapon against the ex-spouse. Vindictiveness is a big problem in divorce situations. The children have now become collateral damage in the battle between the ex-spouses. This also leaves a lot of scars on the lives of the children due to the great potential for unforgiveness. This is how generational curses get passed on. The exes often will attempt to poison the children against the other parent. Ultimately, the children will decide for themselves which parent was telling the truth.

The many sins committed during the months or years that ultimately led to the divorce creates a lot of woundedness which often leads to hostility between the parents. This then often leads to one or both of the parents using the children as weapons against the ex-spouse. The children have now become collateral damage in the battle between the ex-spouses. This also leaves a lot of scars on the lives of the children. This is how generational curses get passed on.

Exodus 20:5
[5] You shall not bow down to them or serve them, for I the LORD your God am a jealous God, visiting the iniquity of the fathers on the children to the third and the fourth generation of those who hate me, (ESV)

The next item to discuss is the impact the divorce has on each person's social life. This is where you have to decide who gets to keep the friends and who gets to keep the pets. This also has a huge impact on the children. When married couples develop a network of married friends, generally everyone is in the same boat. Everyone is considered "safe" and/or "off limits" because everyone is married. However, now that there is one party in the network that is "available", some of the married folks could eventually see the divorced person as either a temptation or a threat. So now, insecurities start to manifest themselves and some people will begin to distance themselves from the divorced person. For the divorced person, their social network often decreases in size. This can lead to feelings of isolation or abandonment which could then lead to depression and other mental health issues.

Humans were created to be in relationship not only with God, but one another. Isolation allows the enemy to easily pick you off and subject you to more severe spiritual attacks. Post-divorce really should be a time of rebuilding your relationship with God (your vertical relationship) as well as your social network (horizontal relationships). Take some time to look back on all the issues that led to the divorce. Take a good look in the mirror and try to remove the log in your eye.

Consider the following Scriptures:

Matthew 7:1–5

Judging Others

[1] "Judge not, that you be not judged.

[2] For with the judgment you pronounce you will be judged, and with the measure you use it will be measured to you.

[3] Why do you see the speck that is in your brother's eye, but do not notice the log that is in your own eye?

[4] Or how can you say to your brother, 'Let me take the speck out of your eye,' when there is the log in your own eye?

[5] You hypocrite, first take the log out of your own eye, and then you will see clearly to take the speck out of your brother's eye. (ESV)

Proverbs 18:1

"Whoever isolates himself seeks his own desire; he breaks out against all sound judgment."

Hebrews 10:25

"Not neglecting to meet together, as is the habit of some, but encouraging one another, and all the more as you see the Day drawing near".

1 Corinthians 12:14

[14] For the body does not consist of one member but of many. (ESV)

The final landmine that we will discuss is the frequent situation where one party has a need to go back to court to alter the original divorce agreement. The most common reasons are to change alimony payments, child support and child custody. The only entities that make out well throughout the various court proceedings are the law firms. So keep in mind, every time you choose to go to court, you are spending money that could have been used for much greater purposes and eventually been the inheritance for your grandkids. The following scripture reinforces the fact that we, as Christians, are to let the Lord fight our battles.

1 Corinthians 6:6–7
[6] but brother goes to law against brother, and that before unbelievers?

[7] To have lawsuits at all with one another is already a defeat for you. Why not rather suffer wrong? Why not rather be defrauded? (ESV)

Luke 12:57-59
Settle with Your Accuser

[57] "And why do you not judge for yourselves what is right?

[58] As you go with your accuser before the magistrate, make an effort to settle with him on the way, lest he drag you to the judge, and the judge hand you over to the officer, and the officer put you in prison.

[59] I tell you, you will never get out until you have paid the very last penny." (ESV)

Romans 12:17
"Repay no one evil for evil, but give thought to do what is honorable in the sight of all." (ESV)

Romans 12:2
"Do not be overcome by evil, but overcome evil with good." (ESV)

Romans 12:19
"Beloved, never avenge yourselves, but leave it to the wrath of God, for it is written, "Vengeance is mine, I will repay, says the Lord." (ESV)

Alimony is generally based on the income of the primary earner as a way to enable the supported spouse to be able to maintain a certain level of existence as in the basics – food, clothing and shelter. The court decides what is "fair and equitable" based on one party's income (at the time) and then dictates what that amount will be. Things to watch out for here, is that many times, the spouse ordered to pay the alimony will deliberately quit a job or even move to a different city or state to try to get out of paying the money ordered by the court. This is part of that spiritual warfare you will have to deal with now that you are under the influence of the law.

1 Timothy 6:10 "For the love of money is a root of all kinds of evils. It is through this craving that some have wandered away from the faith and pierced themselves with many pangs."

Child support is in addition to alimony and is generally required to be paid until the child reaches the age of adulthood, which in the US, is 18 years old. The big landmine here is that even though the divorce decree states that child support is required, many times the party that is supposed to pay it doesn't fulfill that obligation. This usually puts the other spouse in financial jeopardy.

As you see in the scripture above in 1st Timothy 6:10, the LOVE of money is the root of all kinds of evil. In many cases, it was this love of money that led to the divorce in the first place. Alimony and child support payments are often simply not made forcing the other party to spend limited resources to have the court enforce what was already decreed. There are sometimes deliberate behaviors to hide assets or for the person to be "lost" so the courts can't find them to enforce the court orders. This is also part of the reason God hates divorce (Malachi 2:16) is for the damage it does to families by breaking them up. There is usually a lot of unforgiveness that often lasts for many years.

Issues over child custody frequently bring ex-spouses back into the courtroom. A big reason for the need to return to the court system is that one or both of the exes do not live up to the original agreement. Often, this is due to deliberate behavior by one spouse. This is the situation briefly mentioned above. Often out of spite, one spouse will effectively use the child/children as leverage to manipulate the former spouse. The "exchange" dates and times often get changed at the last minute to cause a disruption in the other household's plans.

There is not much worse than a vindictive ex-spouse. An ex, with a vindictive spirit, can cause all sorts of havoc. You are basically living in their head rent free. A person with that kind of spirit will spend most of their time trying to find ways to make your life Hell.

In closing, you will be much better off by rebuilding your vertical relationship and focusing on making God your provider, your protector and your peace. If your focus is on all the issues, the enemy is winning by stealing your peace and causing you lots of unnecessary stress. Let God fight the battles. Romans 12:19 was mentioned earlier, but it needs to be repeated here.

Romans 12:19

"Beloved, never avenge yourselves, but leave it to the wrath of God, for it is written, "Vengeance is mine, I will repay, says the Lord." (ESV)

As you go through the lesson, take time to meditate on the various scriptures and use the next couple of pages to journal your thoughts, feelings and emotions as well as the things God is working on with you.

CHAPTER 10

Preparing for Your New Journey

Because God created us with a need for relationship, eventually you may get tired of living alone and start thinking about the possibilities of a new relationship. Many single parents never heal from the wounds they suffered during the time leading up to the decision to divorce and the time of the actual process of divorce. They spend many years holding on to unforgiveness and end up being the ones to do the most suffering.

There is a good chance you may have made a vow to yourself that you will never get remarried or allow yourself to be hurt by anyone ever again. Since you really have no clue what tomorrow may bring, that vow may come back to haunt you someday. That vow precludes you from truly seeking God's Will because you have attempted to take control of your future. Confess that vow as sin, repent and ask God for His forgiveness. He will set you free from that vow.

> ***James 4:13-15***
> *Boasting About Tomorrow*
>
> *[13] Come now, you who say, "Today or tomorrow we will go into such and such a town and spend a year there and trade and make a profit"—*
>
> *[14] yet you do not know what tomorrow will bring. What is your life? For you are a mist that appears for a little time and then vanishes.*
>
> *[15] Instead you ought to say, "If the Lord wills, we will live and do this or that." (ESV)*

When you have freed yourself from that vow, then God can start working in your life again. Many times, when you have stopped looking for someone to have a relationship with, that's when God brings someone into your life. It's when you least expect it, that new person will 'miraculously" appear in your life.

Since you are here, in this book, at this time, the assumption is that you have done the majority of the work needed to forgive the ex-spouse/co-parent, get closer to God and have reestablished a healthy vertical relationship. There's probably still a little bit of work left to accomplish to really be totally whole again.

God wants all of His children to be whole so that when He multiplies them together, He still gets the one flesh that He desires for a man and a woman in marriage (1 times 1 = 1). When two people that are less than whole try to multiply themselves together in marriage or any other sort of relationship, they are going to be multiplying fractions (½ times ½ = ¼). When fractions are multiplied together, the pieces just keep getting smaller.

It is critical that you take the necessary time you need before jumping into a new relationship to deal with your wounds and be healed. As was mentioned in an earlier lesson, it's also important that any children impacted by the divorce have time to heal. It would be wise to seek counseling for yourself and your children to help them deal with their issues caused by the divorce.

Proverbs 11:13-15

[13] Whoever goes about slandering reveals secrets,
but he who is trustworthy in spirit keeps a thing covered.

[14] Where there is no guidance, a people falls,
but in an abundance of counselors there is safety.

[15] Whoever puts up security for a stranger will surely suffer harm,
but he who hates striking hands in pledge is secure. (ESV)

Preparation for a new relationship is a serious matter. Having been through a divorce, when you finally choose to start over, there is a very high probability that you will be involved with someone else that has also been through a divorce. A first marriage is hard work. A subsequent marriage is even more difficult. If you have not dealt with the issues that caused the divorce, you are doomed to repeat them. Now, because you have been through the process of divorce in the past, it will be easier to simply throw away another relationship when those issues resurface.

Become a student of marriage. Learn what God intended for marriage in the beginning with Adam and Eve. When things get serious with the new relationship, PLEASE make sure BOTH of you go through some classes TOGETHER that are specific to blended families. Blended families are unique in that, in many cases, there will be many external influences (such as vindictive ex-spouses/co-parents) that will be a frequent source of conflict in your new relationship.

If you enter into a blended family with the idea that it will be just like a first marriage, you will find out quickly that there are many more issues to deal with than you ever even had to think about in a first marriage. Once you make the decision to remarry, you will be greatly blessed for years to come if you go through some premarital counseling that deals with blended family issues. You both really need to know where the lands mines are buried.

God established an order for the universe and everything in it. That includes marriage and family as well. When a man and a woman who are believers seek God's Will in bringing a new partner into their life, God makes sure they get the perfect (according to Him) partner. When these two ultimately get married and share their vows in the presence of God, they have entered into a covenant with God and each other. This is a "till death do us part" covenant.

There will be times where you will question whether or not God brought you the right person. There will be times when that new person just really gets under your skin and drives you nuts.

But, in God's perfect wisdom, He will show you that there will also be times when you wonder how you ever survived without them.

Part of the premarital process should be developing with your (soon-to-be) new spouse a road map of where you feel God wants the two of you to go. Without a vision or plan for where you need to go, you will spend a lot of time wandering around in the desert. Determining where God wants to take you on this new road trip will take praying together on a daily basis and then being still and listening for His voice to guide you.

Proverbs 29:18
[18] Where there is no prophetic vision the people cast off restraint,
but blessed is he who keeps the law. (ESV)

Psalm 46:9-11
[9] He makes wars cease to the end of the earth;
he breaks the bow and shatters the spear;
he burns the chariots with fire.

[10] "Be still, and know that I am God.
I will be exalted among the nations,
I will be exalted in the earth!"

[11] The LORD of hosts is with us;
the God of Jacob is our fortress. Selah (ESV)

God wants to have a relationship with you. He loves you unconditionally and wants to prosper you. The ultimate prosperity is being able to spend eternity with Jesus.

Romans 8:38-39
[38] For I am sure that neither death nor life, nor angels nor rulers, nor things present nor things to come, nor powers,

[39] nor height nor depth, nor anything else in all creation, will be able to separate us from the love of God in Christ Jesus our Lord. (ESV)

3 John 1-3
Greeting

[1] The elder to the beloved Gaius, whom I love in truth.

[2] Beloved, I pray that all may go well with you and that you may be in good health, as it goes well with your soul.

[3] For I rejoiced greatly when the brothers came and testified to your truth, as indeed you are walking in the truth. (ESV)

As you go through the lesson, take time to meditate on the various scriptures and use the next couple of pages to journal your thoughts, feelings and emotions as well as the things God is working on with you.

REVIEW SECTION

CHAPTER 11

How Will You Allow God to Pick Your Next Relationship?

By now, you should understand the process you need to go through to let go of the past, receive healing and move "Beyond Divorce".

Have an understanding of what a covenant marriage is so that when God brings someone new into your life, you will be prepared to do what is necessary to make it work in spite of a lack of perfection. Be prepared to extend grace and mercy just as God does for you .Always look for the blessings.

Take responsibility for YOUR actions. Don't play the victim. In Christ, you are already victorious. Each person has to answer to God for themselves. Don't try to carry the whole load of responsibility for what caused the divorce. Each party has to deal with their own stuff.

Learn to be a good forgiver. Also be quick to forgive. This will allow you to free yourself from the spiritual baggage that has been created over the time leading up to the divorce. As you forgive others, it is also required that you forgive yourself. For some, this is difficult depending on what the particular circumstances are. But, realize, that true freedom comes when you no longer hold on to your chains from the past.

Be sure to take time to heal from the wounds created from those things that led to the divorce. Lots of hurtful things get said and done along the way. Go through the grieving steps outlined in a previous chapter. Take the time you need. Don't rush it! It's different for everyone. Remember the words from Ecclesiastes – There is a time for everything. Trust God for your healing. Draw near to Him and He will draw near to you.

Get your vertical relationship back in good standing. This will enable all your other relationships to work at their best. You will feel good about yourself and will be more at peace in your environment. This will then make you more attractive to others as well. Someone that is at peace with themselves has a way of drawing others closer just as God's peace draws us closer to Him.

Are you ready to become a true Christian soldier? When you accepted Christ as your savior, you just enlisted in His army. You were not drafted. You are in the Army now! Why else would God give you a suit of armor to wear? He has missions for you to go on to increase the size of

His kingdom. You now have a target on your back, so be prepared to do spiritual battle with the true enemy of your soul. At this point, post-divorce, you should be able to go back in time and see where the enemy took some of your territory. Learn the lessons, but don't continue to live there in the past.

Understand that God created humans in His image and also to have relationship with Him. Our relationship with Him is lived out here on Earth by having relationships with each other, Not in all cases, but in most, you will, at some point, desire to have a life partner once again. Make sure you are ready. Pray and tell God what you desire in a new spouse. Be very sure you are whole now and that the person God brings to your attention is whole. You are not in the fix and flip business. You need to be looking for move-in ready. God likes to multiply whole numbers. From math class, we know 1x1=1. That's How God does it. He will take a whole "you" and multiply you with another whole "one" and get the one flesh unit that He desires. If you are not whole, DO NOT try to start a relationship. When you multiply fractions, the pieces get smaller.

Be healed, be whole and don't be "needy". Be OK with yourself so that you can function with only your vertical relationship. THEN – you are ready for new horizontal relationships. The last thing you need going forward is to be in a co-dependent relationship. As was just discussed, work on yourself so that as you receive God's blessings from above to excess, you will be full and you can let the overflow pour out onto you loved ones without needing anything in return.

Transform your mind to be more like Christ. Romans 12:2 "Do not be conformed to this world, but be transformed by the renewal of your mind, that by testing you may discern what is the will of God, what is good and acceptable and perfect." In the NKJV, In Proverbs 23:7 You will see that as a man thinks, that is how he will be. He will do what he thinks about. Do you think about what you think about? In 2nd Corinthians 10:5 the scripture says to take every thought captive. Are you familiar with the phrase "on second thought"? This is that scripture in action. You have a thought, you take it captive, you run it through your Jesus filter and then decide if it's ok, or whether you should discard it and have a second thought to replace it.

Trust God with your future – He has one for you (Jeremiah 29:11). As the scripture says, there is a future and a hope that God has for us. God knows our past, but he also knows our future. Satan only knows our past. When we are faithful to confess our sins, God is faithful to forgive our sins AND he forgets. We do not have the ability to forget the way God does. I believe that is so that you will learn from your mistakes. If you could forget the past mistakes the way God does, you would never learn any lessons. You might consider that because God forgets about your sins and remembers them no more, that in a sense, your past is irrelevant to God. He is your today and your tomorrow. Satan cares about your past because that's what he will throw in your face every chance he gets.

Get filled from above (Jesus), so that you can pour out into others.

James 1:16–18

[16] Do not be deceived, my beloved brothers.

[17] Every good gift and every perfect gift is from above, coming down from the Father of lights, with whom there is no variation or shadow due to change.

[18] Of his own will he brought us forth by the word of truth, that we should be a kind of firstfruits of his creatures. (ESV)

Imagine being the first one up in the morning and you make a fresh pot of coffee (which we will call love). You pour yourself a cup of love. You are feeling very good right now. Then the rest of the family starts to arrive in the kitchen. For this example, there is no spouse right now. They all want some love too. But since you are the single parent, you decide to give away some of your love out of your cup. After two or three servings of love from your cup, now your cup is nearly empty. So what do you do now? Obviously, you need to refill your cup from the pot. But the trick here is that your cup should be getting filled from above and as God is pouring out His blessings on you He is pouring them out to capacity and to overflowing. So as God's blessings are spilling over, you can stay full, and your overflow can be poured out on to your loved ones. If you keep giving your love away without getting refilled from above, you will run out and will not have any to give.

Set healthy boundaries. Don't allow the negative back into your life. God's will is to restore and to reconcile as it says in

<u>Amos 9:11–12</u>
The Restoration of Israel

[11] "In that day I will raise up the booth of David that is fallen and repair its breaches,and raise up its ruins and rebuild it as in the days of old,

[12] that they may possess the remnant of Edom and all the nations who are called by my name," declares the LORD who does this. (ESV)

God will restore what the enemy has stolen and destroyed. He will reconcile His people to Himself. That's your vertical Relationship. Your horizontal ones are not always possible to restore or reconcile. It is often necessary to put boundaries in place between you and your ex, or anyone else that may have a toxic influence on you. As you have learned, you are to love your enemies, but sometimes it is necessary to love them from some distance. If a person constantly hurts you, you need to establish a healthy boundary between them and you. This is for your own protection – physical and emotional.

Refuse to pick up bricks of offense. (Read "The Bait of Satan" by John Bevere). I highly recommend that you read this book. It has a very profound explanation of how the enemy uses "being offended" as a favorite tool of the enemy to get the body of Christ "eating its own". Choosing to pick up and then carrying an offense, rather than forgiving it right away, becomes like a cancer in the body of Christ. People start judging each other which opens the door to the enemy to bring more accusations against the brethren. You also have the choice to not pick up an offence by extending grace from the start.

Don't go hunting for a new relationship. Let God be God. He will bring someone when you're ready. Your job during this season of new beginnings is to work on yourself. Become the "you" that God wants you to be. One of the best nuggets of marital advice that can be given is that "God is not in the spouse changing business. He's in the YOU changing business."

Luke 6:39–42

[39] He also told them a parable: "Can a blind man lead a blind man? Will they not both fall into a pit?

[40] A disciple is not above his teacher, but everyone when he is fully trained will be like his teacher.

[41] Why do you see the speck that is in your brother's eye, but do not notice the log that is in your own eye?

[42] How can you say to your brother, 'Brother, let me take out the speck that is in your eye,' when you yourself do not see the log that is in your own eye? You hypocrite, first take the log out of your own eye, and then you will see clearly to take out the speck that is in your brother's eye. (ESV)

No Fear! – Enjoy the journey. You should already know your destination. When you really grasp the concept of eternal life in Heaven, this life here on Earth, should be one you look forward to escaping at some point. While you are hear, do what you can for the glory of God. Your reward will be eternity in Heaven.

Philippians 1:18–26

To Live Is Christ

Yes, and I will rejoice,

[19] for I know that through your prayers and the help of the Spirit of Jesus Christ this will turn out for my deliverance,

[20] as it is my eager expectation and hope that I will not be at all ashamed, but that with full courage now as always Christ will be honored in my body, whether by life or by death. [21] For to me to live is Christ, and to die is gain.

[22] If I am to live in the flesh, that means fruitful labor for me. Yet which I shall choose I cannot tell.

[23] I am hard pressed between the two. My desire is to depart and be with Christ, for that is far better.

[24] But to remain in the flesh is more necessary on your account.

[25] Convinced of this, I know that I will remain and continue with you all, for your progress and joy in the faith, [26] so that in me you may have ample cause to glory in Christ Jesus, because of my coming to you again. (ESV)

Dream Big – Have a Vision – Set Goals.

Proverbs 29:18 "18 Where there is no prophetic vision the people cast off restraint, but blessed is he who keeps the law". (ESV)

This phrase is frequently quoted as "without vision my people perish". What the scripture describes is that without clear goals or a defined purpose, people tend to become ungovernable and refuse to be reined in. The quote is often used to emphasize the importance of having a vision or goal in life. The vision is provided by God, and his prophets relayed this vision to the people. A few scriptures are referenced below to encourage you in your new season.

Proverbs 21:5
The plans of the diligent lead surely to abundance, but everyone who is hasty comes only to poverty. (ESV)

Habakkuk 2:2-3
[2]And the Lord answered me: "Write the vision; make it plain on tablets, so he may run who reads it.

[3]For still the vision awaits its appointed time; it hastens to the end—it will not lie. If it seems slow, wait for it; it will surely come; it will not delay. (ESV)

Philippians 3:13–14
[13] Brothers, I do not consider that I have made it my own. But one thing I do: forgetting what lies behind and straining forward to what lies ahead,

[14] I press on toward the goal for the prize of the upward call of God in Christ Jesus. (ESV)

2 Chronicles 15:7
But you, take courage! Do not let your hands be weak, for your work shall be rewarded." (ESV)

Proverbs 24:27
Prepare your work outside; get everything ready for yourself in the field, and after that build your house. (ESV)

Luke 14:28

For which of you, desiring to build a tower, does not first sit down and count the cost, whether he has enough to complete it? (ESV)

Proverbs 3:5-6

Trust in the Lord with all your heart, and do not lean on your own understanding. In all your ways acknowledge him, and he will make straight your paths. (ESV)

Isaiah 54:2

"Enlarge the place of your tent, and let the curtains of your habitations be stretched out; do not hold back; lengthen your cords and strengthen your stakes. (ESV)

Proverbs 16:9

The heart of man plans his way, but the Lord establishes his steps. (ESV)

James 4:13–15

Boasting About Tomorrow

[13] Come now, you who say, "Today or tomorrow we will go into such and such a town and spend a year there and trade and make a profit"—

[14] yet you do not know what tomorrow will bring. What is your life? For you are a mist that appears for a little time and then vanishes.

[15] Instead you ought to say, "If the Lord wills, we will live and do this or that." (ESV)

Matthew 21:22

And whatever you ask in prayer, you will receive, if you have faith." (ESV)

Matthew 6:33 l

But seek first the kingdom of God and his righteousness, and all these things will be added to you. (ESV)

As you go through the lesson, take time to meditate on the various scriptures and use the next couple of pages to journal your thoughts, feelings and emotions as well as the things God is working on with you.

CHAPTER 12

Are You Still Struggling in any Areas?

As we begin to wrap up this class, there are a few things we need to revisit at this time. This class deals with the process of healing from past hurts and moving on and that process is different for each individual, so this would be a good time to see if there are any issues that still need to be addressed.

You have been taught about God's plan for marriage, taking responsibility for YOUR part of what brought about the divorce, forgiveness, the necessity of taking time to heal, how to repair your vertical relationship with God, how to be ready to hear God's voice, how to get ready for your new season, communication skills, how to avoid the post-divorce landmines and how to navigate the seven stages of grief. This is a good time for you to take a look in the mirror, take inventory and really look deep into YOU. The goal here, is for you to experience the freedom and peace that comes from the healing that Jesus provides. Let's go through the following checklist to see how you are doing in some of the most important areas of understanding the principles and assessing your current level of healing.

Things that might still be difficult to obtain and/or maintain…

Forgiveness of self or others –

Spend some time with the Lord and ask him to reveal to you if there is anyone that you might need to forgive or anything that you might need to be forgiven for. Perhaps there is someone that you need to ask for forgiveness. The most important person to forgive is you. If you have gone to God and confessed your sins, God is faithful to forgive your sins AND forgets about it. Remember, if God has forgiven you, if you don't forgive yourself, you are putting yourself higher than God. Forgiveness is mandatory. Reconciliation is optional. God's will is for restoration and reconciliation.

> ***Matthew 6:15*** *"but if you do not forgive others their trespasses, neither will your Father forgive your trespasses." (ESV)*
>
> ***Romans 12:18*** *If possible, so far as it depends on you, live peaceably with all. (ESV)*

Vertical relationship -

The vertical relationship is your personal relationship with Christ. Do you feel that it is in good order? Are you spending time with him every day? Do you feel his presence? Is Jesus your main focus or are you still getting distracted by things from the past? Is there anything in your life that is preventing you from developing a strong connection with the Holy Spirit? This is your opportunity to again take a serious look in the mirror to assess your heart and let God reveal any hidden problems or unhealed wounds that still need attention. Be sure to get the Word in you so you can recognize the lies from the real enemy. The enemy frequently twists the scripture ever so slightly so that it sounds right to the uninformed, but actually will mislead you into error. Psalm 51 is a great roadmap on how to restore your vertical relationship.

Psalm 51

"Create in Me a Clean Heart, O God

To the choirmaster. A Psalm of David, when Nathan the prophet went to him, after he had gone in to Bathsheba.

51 Have mercy on me, O God,
according to your steadfast love;
according to your abundant mercy
blot out my transgressions.
2 Wash me thoroughly from my iniquity,
and cleanse me from my sin!
3 For I know my transgressions,
and my sin is ever before me.
4 Against you, you only, have I sinned
and done what is evil in your sight,
so that you may be justified in your words
and blameless in your judgment.
5 Behold, I was brought forth in iniquity,
and in sin did my mother conceive me.
6 Behold, you delight in truth in the inward being,
and you teach me wisdom in the secret heart.
7 Purge me with hyssop, and I shall be clean;
wash me, and I shall be whiter than snow.
8 Let me hear joy and gladness;
let the bones that you have broken rejoice.
9 Hide your face from my sins,
and blot out all my iniquities.
10 Create in me a clean heart, O God,
and renew a right spirit within me.
11 Cast me not away from your presence,
and take not your Holy Spirit from me.
12 Restore to me the joy of your salvation,
and uphold me with a willing spirit.
13 Then I will teach transgressors your ways,
and sinners will return to you.
14 Deliver me from bloodguiltiness, O God,
O God of my salvation,
and my tongue will sing aloud of your righteousness.
15 O Lord, open my lips,
and my mouth will declare your praise.
16 For you will not delight in sacrifice, or I would give it;
you will not be pleased with a burnt offering.
17 The sacrifices of God are a broken spirit;
a broken and contrite heart, O God, you will not despise.
18 Do good to Zion in your good pleasure;
build up the walls of Jerusalem;

[19] then will you delight in right sacrifices,
in burnt offerings and whole burnt offerings;
then bulls will be offered on your altar." *(ESV)*

Your identity in Christ –

Do you identify the most with what you have done, what's been to you, or do you identify with who you belong to? Satan is the accuser, but he can only accuse you of sins that have not been forgiven. Unforgiven sins, which often are the result of trauma from your younger days, are what Satan uses to accuse you if those fiery darts are still present for him to grab and throw at you.

> ***2 Corinthians 5:17*** *"Therefore, if anyone is in Christ, he is a new creation. The old has passed away; behold, the new has come." (ESV)*

This scripture is to remind you that your history, no matter how messed up it may have been, has been cleansed of all unrighteousness and you are now reborn. You are now covered by the blood of Jesus with His righteousness imputed to you.

Prayer/Fasting –

Nehemiah 1:4
Nehemiah's Prayer

[4] As soon as I heard these words I sat down and wept and mourned for days, and I continued fasting and praying before the God of heaven. (ESV)

Matthew 6:16
Fasting

[16] "And when you fast, do not look gloomy like the hypocrites, for they disfigure their faces that their fasting may be seen by others. Truly, I say to you, they have received their reward. (ESV)

ALL THINGS are possible through Christ –

Now that you have been working on your vertical relationship, it's time to put your faith to work.

James 2:14–17
Faith Without Works Is Dead

[14] What good is it, my brothers, if someone says he has faith but does not have works? Can that faith save him?

[15] If a brother or sister is poorly clothed and lacking in daily food,

[16] and one of you says to them, "Go in peace, be warmed and filled," without giving them the things needed for the body, what good is that?

[17] So also faith by itself, if it does not have works, is dead. (ESV)

In Matthew 19:26 you will find that with God's help, you can do or get through anything.

Matthew 19:26
[26] But Jesus looked at them and said, "With man this is impossible, but with God all things are possible." (ESV)

Press through the hard times with God's strength –

One of the most recognizable scriptures to help you get through tough times is the following –

Philippians 4:13 *"I can do all things through him who strengthens me." (ESV)*

Let's look at a few more scriptures. There are many more you can find in your own reading time. Your personal study time will reveal many things as you spend time with the Lord.

Isaiah 41:10 *"Fear not, for I am with you; be not dismayed, for I am your God; I will strengthen you, I will help you, I will uphold you with my righteous right hand."* ***(ESV)***

Ephesians 6:10 *"Finally, be strong in the Lord and in the strength of his might."* ***(ESV)***

Isaiah 40:31 *"But they who wait for the Lord shall renew their strength; they shall mount up with wings like eagles; they shall run and not be weary; they shall walk and not faint."* ***(ESV)***

Exodus 15:2 *"The Lord is my strength and my song, and he has become my salvation; this is my God, and I will praise him, my father's God, and I will exalt him."* ***(ESV)***

Trust in God in times of trouble. He is your strength during times of trials and tribulations.

Be aware of the Spiritual Warfare going on around you-

This is one of the most important areas to understand. Life in general is spiritual warfare. Marriage in particular is spiritual warfare. When you and/or your spouse are unaware of who the real enemy is, you will end up being a casualty of the warfare. Ephesians 6 gives you what you need to know as well as the equipment needed to be successful in winning the battles.

> **Ephesians 6:10–20**
> *The Whole Armor of God*
>
> *[10] Finally, be strong in the Lord and in the strength of his might.*
>
> *[11] Put on the whole armor of God, that you may be able to stand against the schemes of the devil.*
>
> *[12] For we do not wrestle against flesh and blood, but against the rulers, against the authorities, against the cosmic powers over this present darkness, against the spiritual forces of evil in the heavenly places.*
>
> *[13] Therefore take up the whole armor of God, that you may be able to withstand in the evil day, and having done all, to stand firm.*
>
> *[14] Stand therefore, having fastened on the belt of truth, and having put on the breastplate of righteousness,*
>
> *[15] and, as shoes for your feet, having put on the readiness given by the gospel of peace.*
>
> *[16] In all circumstances take up the shield of faith, with which you can extinguish all the flaming darts of the evil one;*
>
> *[17] and take the helmet of salvation, and the sword of the Spirit, which is the word of God,*
>
> *[18] praying at all times in the Spirit, with all prayer and supplication. To that end, keep alert with all perseverance, making supplication for all the saints,*
>
> *[19] and also for me, that words may be given to me in opening my mouth boldly to proclaim the mystery of the gospel,*
>
> *[20] for which I am an ambassador in chains, that I may declare it boldly, as I ought to speak. (ESV)*

Be free from past sins (Through forgiveness) – Satan wants to keep you in bondage.

One of my favorite sayings, which is really fairly simple, but very deep when you really think about it. It really shows the difference in how your Father wants to bless you and the enemy want to take you out! When you confess yours sins to God, they are wiped away. Then, there is nothing left for Satan to accuse you of.

Satan knows your name, but calls you by your sin.

God knows your sin, but calls you by your name.

It's important to understand that Satan is the real enemy. He lies. As Revelation says, he is the accuser of the bretheren.

Revelation 12:10

[10] And I heard a loud voice in heaven, saying, "Now the salvation and the power and the kingdom of our God and the authority of his Christ have come, for the accuser of our brothers has been thrown down, who accuses them day and night before our God. (ESV)

Think about "pre-forgiveness – The idea of forgiving people BEFORE they offend you, especially when you know they will.

In Luke 15, the parable of the prodigal son, at the point where the son finally returns to the father, the father runs to meet his son. After the hurtful things the son did to the father, once the father saw the son, he didn't have to stop and think about having to forgive him at that point in time. The father had already forgiven the son quite some time ago. He was just so happy to see him come home. So, when you have someone in your family or a co-worker that just really rubs you the wrong way, try forgiving the ahead of time if you are sure they will do something to offend you when you see them. This is a good time to remember Christ on the cross when He said, "Father, forgive them, for they know not what they do".

Renewed Thinking - Follow the Holy Spirit

Galatian 5:1 "For freedom Christ has set us free; stand firm therefore, and do not submit again to a yoke of slavery."

Galatians 5:16–26

Keep in Step with the Spirit

[16] But I say, walk by the Spirit, and you will not gratify the desires of the flesh.

[17] For the desires of the flesh are against the Spirit, and the desires of the Spirit are against the flesh, for these are opposed to each other, to keep you from doing the things you want to do.

[18] But if you are led by the Spirit, you are not under the law.

[19] Now the works of the flesh are evident: sexual immorality, impurity, sensuality,

[20] idolatry, sorcery, enmity, strife, jealousy, fits of anger, rivalries, dissensions, divisions,

[21] envy, drunkenness, orgies, and things like these. I warn you, as I warned you before, that those who do such things will not inherit the kingdom of God.

[22] But the fruit of the Spirit is love, joy, peace, patience, kindness, goodness, faithfulness,

[23] gentleness, self-control; against such things there is no law.

[24] And those who belong to Christ Jesus have crucified the flesh with its passions and desires.

[25] If we live by the Spirit, let us also keep in step with the Spirit.

[26] Let us not become conceited, provoking one another, envying one another. (ESV)

Love your Enemies – Bless them that curse you

In the Old Testament (Leviticus 24:16-18) justice was an "eye for an eye". Today, in the New Testament, in Matthew 5:38 a reference is made to the Old Testament scripture of "an eye for an eye" before we get the newer updated version.

Matthew 5:43–48
Love Your Enemies

43] "You have heard that it was said, 'You shall love your neighbor and hate your enemy.'

[44] But I say to you, Love your enemies and pray for those who persecute you,

[45] so that you may be sons of your Father who is in heaven. For he makes his sun rise on the evil and on the good, and sends rain on the just and on the unjust. [46] For if you love those who love you, what reward do you have? Do not even the tax collectors do the same?

[47] And if you greet only your brothers, what more are you doing than others? Do not even the Gentiles do the same?

[48] You therefore must be perfect, as your heavenly Father is perfect. (ESV)

As you go through the lesson, take time to meditate on the various scriptures and use the next couple of pages to journal your thoughts, feelings and emotions as well as the things God is working on with you.

Printed in the United States
by Baker & Taylor Publisher Services

Printed in the United States
by Baker & Taylor Publisher Services